21874

Royal Mail Stamps

David Gentleman's designs for the Liverpool–Manchester Railway issue of March 1980

STUART ROSE

Royal Mail Stamps
a survey of British stamp design

PHAIDON

Phaidon Press Limited, Littlegate House,
St Ebbe's Street, Oxford

© Phaidon Press Limited 1980

ISBN 0 7148 2072 5

Printed in Great Britain by Jolly & Barber Ltd, Rugby

Contents

Preface

Being neither a philatelist nor a stamp collector in the accepted meaning, I can claim little of the philatelic expertise normally essential to the writing of a book about stamps. But as a graphic designer, and one who has spent many years in the Post Office being involved in the direction of stamp design, I do claim a professional view of the design content of a stamp as being a highly significant ingredient in the total philatelic mix and therefore of the utmost importance to the stamp collector.

I have made little attempt to advance my own views on the difference between good and not so good design. But I have tried to show how influences, both on the Post Office and by the Post Office, do have a fundamental effect on the final result; and I have tried to distinguish the good from the bad. If in so doing I have been able to give those whose prime interest is philately, and even those for whom it is not, a deeper insight into this fascinating subject then the book will have done its job.

Certainly its publication has only been made possible by the willing help I have received from many of my friends in the Post Office, particularly in the National Postal Museum and from the staff in the Marketing Department in Postal Headquarters, who are responsible for the design and production of stamps. Nor must I forget the help in having access to the Stamp Committee papers at the Design Council and to the Sir Francis Meynell archive, now housed in the Cambridge University Library.

I also owe gratitude to those designers, with whom I have worked in the past, for their readiness to give me their own views on a number of questions which a study of this kind inevitably raises, and also for allowing me to reproduce some of their original material. And lastly, to Dodo my wife, who has spent many tiresome hours translating my illegible longhand into (in her words) mis-typed copy and a confusion of taped interviews into semi-readable sense.

Stuart Rose
4 October 1979

Opposite: The experimental designs by Edmund Dulac which led to one of the stamps used in the Coronation issue of June 1953 (see also page 78)

Design Council Award 1973

British Pictorial Stamps of 1972

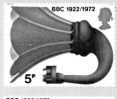

1/1 The 1972 stamps which won the Design Council Award in 1973

1 Postage stamps: industrial design or fine art?

In June 1973 the Post Office received from the Design Council a Design Award for the previous year's issues of postage stamps. The award was made, not for the philatelic or fine art qualities of the stamps, but because of their excellence as examples of graphic design. 'The most unusual award this year' wrote *Design* magazine, 'recognises the work of the Post Office Stamp Advisory Committee and marks a refreshing approach to design combined with an obvious care in co-ordinating not only all the stamps within each issue, but also the first day covers and packs of mint stamps. This resulted in a consistently high standard of design combined with an interesting variety of graphic styles.' It was also the first occasion on which a Design Council award had been made for print.

For the Design Council, whose standards of design are high and demanding, to have made such an award was praise enough. But more important was its recognition that a postage stamp is primarily an example of industrial design, rather than of fine art. Here indeed was justification of the Post Office policy towards stamp design and production which it had been promoting for a number of years.

This is, of course, by no means a popularly held view of stamps, which are generally regarded as applications of miniaturist art rather than of industrial design. But in the eyes of the Post Office stamps play a highly significant part in the handling and trafficking of mail and therefore their design may very properly be judged first on their functional performance and then on their artistic merit. Whatever the Post Office or the public

1/2 First day cover for the Great Britons issue of 1974; see also pp. 105–6

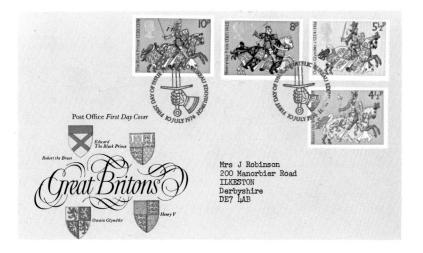

may wish a stamp to do, if it fails to function operationally, it fails utterly.

If then the functional role of the stamp is accepted as being of prime importance, what are the factors which influence its design and production, and how significant are they in determining the ultimate result?

Broadly speaking, there are four main areas of influence imposed respectively by the operational requirements of mail handling, by the choice of subject, by the standard of performance of the designer, and by the technical ability of the printer. All these factors have, in varying degrees, influenced the design and production of stamps since the introduction of the Penny Black in 1840 and they are as important today as they were then.

First then the operational requirements. It must be admitted from the outset that, important as these requirements are for very obvious reasons, they have never been so punitive as to make a good design unattainable. Naturally there have been occasions when a preliminary design had to be amended to meet an operational need, but that sort of situation is in the nature of all industrial design. To coin a well-worn phrase 'design is problem solving' and in postage stamp design the basic problem is to ensure the speedy and certain traffic of mail. Everything else comes after that.

Insofar as a postage stamp is the receipt for the prepayment of a postal service, it becomes the only indication to postal staff of the service that has been bought. It is essential therefore that it should indicate that service in as clear and unambiguous a way as possible. It does so by using numerals and where possible by supporting that identification through the use of unconfusing colours

There was a time between the wars and immediately after, when the Universal Postal Union standardized the colours used to identify comparable services, so that, for example, the colour for European air services to the USA from whatever country was the same. An admirable idea, but the rate of stamp inflation and the increase in the number of multi-coloured stamps made it impossible for the scheme to continue to operate. In 1951 it was abandoned.

For overseas mail the stamp must denote the country of origin. Traditionally, since the first Penny Black, the United Kingdom stamps have always been identified by the Sovereign's effigy which has appeared in varying sizes on every stamp ever issued. Furthermore, at the Post Office counter the clerk must be able to identify the value quickly and with certainty and the customers must also be in no doubt that they've got what they paid for.

Today an increasing volume of mail is being sorted mechanically by means of an electronically-motivated device which reacts to a signal

1/3 Machin definitive and the traditional identification of British stamps by the Sovereign's head: an unambiguous use of numerals, colours and effigy

reflected from the phosphor bands printed on the stamp or contained in the coating of the paper. The strength of the signal depends to a very large extent on the colour over which the phosphor is printed, being stronger at the purple end of the spectrum and weaker at the yellow end. Also a better result is obtained when the tonal value of the colour is light rather than dark. This problem only becomes acute where the design calls for large flat areas of a colour that is unsuitable. When the pattern is broken up by lighter tones, the dominant colour is less likely to cause difficulty, but the need still remains for the designer to hold this operational requirement well to the forefront of his mind.

Perhaps at this stage it would be as well to consider the two categories of stamps that are issued by the Post Office, for the influences that affect the design of all stamps generally are not necessarily common to both types.

First then, let us look at the everyday stamps or what the Post Office and philatelists refer to as 'definitives' or the permanent issues. In the main they are non-representational, the design by tradition being composed of a framework within which is placed the Sovereign's effigy. The current definitives are the first, since the single issue in 1936, to be devoid of any

1/4 Some of the current definitives: the design relies solely on the numeral and the Queen's portrait

1/5 & 6 A line-engraved high
value definitive (1969) and the
1912 seahorse design

decoration, the design relying solely on the Queen's portrait and the value
numeral. Their function is to provide the public with as many variations in
monetary value as to allow for the cost of any service, national and
international, to be met exactly.

Today there are 21 values in circulation and they are available all the
year round at all post offices. The philatelic interest in them, by and large,
is technical rather than aesthetic, consideration being given to such mys-
teries as changes in printing plate or cylinder numbers, differences between graphite or phosphor overprints on the front, types of adhesive on
the back and watermarks in between. They have also contributed their
share of fun to the philatelic game of seek and hide, providing the oc-
casional opportunity for collectors to acquire some erroneous examples. It
has always seemed to me rather ironical that, whereas the Post Office will
spend endless time, money and energy in the pursuit of perfection, the
collector, in his quest for oddities, mistakes and imperfections, sustains a
highly prosperous trade. Certainly there is no other corner in the printer's
world where his errors are sought after with such avidity and with such a
resultant financial gain.

Operationally these stamps are highly sensitive as they account for by far
the greatest volume of mail. Any design defect likely to cause embarrass-
ment in the sorting of mail, either mechanically or by hand, would
therefore have disastrous effects.

For wholly administrative reasons, the issue has always been made in
two parts, in high and low values, and this distinction has been reflected in
the difference in their size, the high values being slightly larger. It has also
provided an interesting comment on relative money values, showing how
quickly in recent years high has become low. In 1970 the 10s value was
issued in the high category while in 1977 the 50p was re-issued as a low
value.

Up until 1977 the high values had been printed by intaglio or what the
stamp trade calls line-engraved recess, whilst the low values were printed
by photogravure. The increased cost of printing and the comparatively
longer time taken to produce the high values ultimately persuaded the Post
Office to abandon the traditional process and have them printed in two
colours by photogravure.

There was no good operational reason for this difference in process, its
motivation being, I suspect, a nostalgic one and perhaps also an opportunity to satisfy the more traditional elements in the philatelic world who
had never really accepted the more commercial-looking process of photogravure. For them line-engraved recess printing spelt quality and they

1/7 & 8 The 1939 Dulac 2s 6d and the Bellew 10s stamp issued in the same year

were prepared to forgive the Post Office, to some extent, for such a falling from philatelic grace if it were to continue to issue some values by the same process that produced the Penny Black.

In some respects I sympathize with this point of view and indeed it is not difficult to point to some lovely stamps printed by that process. But they tend to be found amongst the historic classics in which the design, if I may so stretch the term to embrace the craft skills of the engraver and printer, exploits the technique. It is more difficult to find contemporary stamps of comparable design qualities reproduced by that medium, even if one is to look to the Continent or the United States where the craft of engraving has lived and prospered longer than in this country.

Traditionally the design of high values has always differed from that of the remainder of the issue, but it was not until 1912 with the sea horse design that the Post Office made such a fundamental break with the non-representational framed patterns. In many respects this is a remarkable stamp and very much a product of its time, surpassed only, in my view, by the 1939 issue of Edmund Dulac and the Hon. George Bellew, then Somerset Herald, which have about them, particularly the 2s 6d and the 10s, an unmistakable sense of quality and authority.

But the outstanding high value issue is the Castles set designed by Lynton Lamb and issued between 1955 and 1958.

Perhaps it was just as well that the last high value issues to be produced by this process in 1970 were not up to the standard of craftmanship of some of their predecessors, for when the first two-colour photogravure stamps appeared in 1977, they could well be acclaimed for what they were, really beautiful stamps.

The second category of stamp is variously described as commemorative, special or even pictorial. They are issued from time to time to commemorate a person, an event or an organization or, more recently, as part of the considered Post Office marketing policy to increase both the number of collectors of UK stamps and the volume of sales to existing ones.

Operationally they must conform to the same standards of ability to avoid confusion as do the definitives, but the problem can be aggravated, particularly for Post Office staff, by the fact that they are only in use for a relatively short time and therefore they are less familiar visually than the definitives.

So far as the designer is concerned, the main problem is that posed by the subject itself; indeed the whole question of subject matter is often at the heart of a design solution and it can influence the design quite dramatically for good or ill.

1/9 The Castles high value stamps designed by Lynton Lamb and issued from 1955–58

1/10 One of the first two-colour photogravure high value stamps which appeared in 1977

Over the years Post Office policy towards special issues has changed considerably not only in the selection of subjects, but also in the number and frequency of issues. Design policy too has undergone a fundamental change over the past ten years, a change which brought British stamp design and production to a high place in the world stamps league.

In the course of a year the Post Office may receive up to two hundred requests from outside sources to produce a special issue. Its own marketing department too will prepare a list of subjects which it considers of sufficient importance in terms of public acceptability and political expediency.

The job of reconciliation is perhaps the most taxing part of the stamps production game, for not only must the final programme seem fair and just, but the subjects included in it must themselves be capable of a good design solution. The ultimate quality of stamp design depends as much on the choice of subject as it does on the skill of the designer.

It is not easy to generalize on what is a good and what is a bad subject, although I would put high on the list an inherent sense of dignity and authority and at the bottom triviality.

Speaking to the International Philatelic Congress in Madrid in 1975 I ventured to say: 'We are expected, too, to take some heed of what our marketing people would have us believe to be suitable subjects, but if they had it all their own way babies, dogs, pop stars and football players would be the ideal subjects; all of them admirable and wholly lovable in their own way, but not, I think, the best material for a postage stamp.'

Unintentionally prophetic words, looking at some of the more recent issues from the Post Office!

The prime responsibility for recommending a year's programme of issues lies with the Postal Marketing Department, which also controls design and production. Before sending his proposals up the line to the Postal Management board, and ultimately to the Chairman of the Corporation, the Marketing Director will discuss possible subjects with the Stamp Advisory Committee, of which he is Chairman.

This is a useful stage in the rather long process of programme building as it allows for a wide range of views to be expressed on the basic question of policy, a function more suited to the Committee than the judgement they will ultimately be expected to make on design. At the same time the suitability of the subject to a good design solution will also be discussed with the Design Adviser, although there have been occasions when insufficient consideration has been given to this most important factor. For not all subjects, however worthy in themselves and however good the designer, will necessarily make a good design.

1/11 Two examples of commemorative stamps

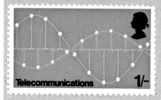

1/12 The 1969 Post Office issue

1/13 & 14 *Right, top and centre:*
the two mixed anniversaries
issues which appeared in 1968
and 1969: the stamps are
unrelated in subject and
inconsistent in design (see
p. 17)

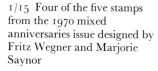

1/15 Four of the five stamps
from the 1970 mixed
anniversaries issue designed by
Fritz Wegner and Marjorie
Saynor

1/16 Two of the four stamps in the 1972 BBC issue

1/17 The Year of the Child issue: the wrong solution?

1/18 & 19 The 1976 issue celebrating the centenary of Graham Bell's telephone and the 1978 Energy issue: a wrong brief and a right solution

Oddly enough, advice on the Post Office's stamp-issuing policy is not included in the official terms of reference for the Committee even though it exists primarily to advise on the implementation of that policy.

There was a time when, in an attempt to include as many different anniversaries as possible, one issue would be made covering a number of events, all different. The first issue was made in 1968 with the TUC centenary, the fiftieth anniversary of women's franchise, the fiftieth birthday of the RAF and the two hundredth anniversary of Captain Cook's first voyage of discovery. A very odd mixture with nothing in common between the four subjects. Another such issue was made the following year with five even more disparate subjects. Admittedly two of them were connected with air flight: Alcock and Brown's Atlantic flight and the first England to Australia flight, both in 1919. But how to integrate them with the International Labour Organization, NATO and the Council for European Posts and Telegraphs? The answer of course was they were not, nor indeed was any attempt made to achieve a consistent design pattern, even though only two designers were involved. Again only two designers' work had been used the year before.

The idea of consistency throughout an issue was not regarded then as being of great importance and indeed out of something like fifty issues, which had been made over the previous twenty years or so, only in twelve of them is there evidence of a conscious design relationship between all the stamps, even when the issues were on the same subject.

There were two reasons for this. First the habit of commissioning more than one designer, and secondly the absence of any design direction over their proposals. Submissions from a number of designers would be placed before the Committee who would then choose those they considered to be the best to make up the required number. The result would inevitably be a mixture of individually good designs, but without any formality in the set.

Very soon that policy was to change with the appointment of a Design Director who could exercise greater control over the development of an issue, and indeed the next mixed anniversaries issue in 1970 proved the success of this new approach. Two designers, Fritz Wegner and Marjorie Saynor, were commissioned to work together on the five subjects with a very tight brief to illustrate each anniversary with the people who were involved in it. The result is a set of five charming designs all closely related to each other in style and form.

Two more such issues were made in 1971 and 1972 neither of which were so successful as the 1970 one and after that the idea of mixed subject issues was fortunately dropped.

Important as the right choice of subject undoubtedly is, it is the way in which the Post Office envisages the ultimate design that will have the most critical effect on the stamp. It must be quite clear in its own mind what the real problem is and how it believes the public will react to a particular point of view expressed by the design. Let me take an example.

Christmas may be expressed visually either as a great big children's party with toys, crackers and Father Christmas; or as a sentimental picture of an England which, I suspect, never really existed, with stage coaches, deep snow, fat jovial welcoming innkeepers and a roaring fire inside a half-timbered coaching inn; or as a religious festival seen through the eyes of a mediaevalist; or as the Sunday School version of a rather different Palestinian scene.

All these options are open to the Post Office and to the designer and each one could be seen by the public as representing current Post Office thinking and policy. Unless therefore the Post Office is quite clear about its own attitude towards a problem, it is unlikely that the designer will be able to create an appropriate design.

Inevitably in the past mistakes have been made by the wrong interpretation being put on a subject and therefore the ultimate design not expressing the subject in the most logical manner. Perhaps the worst example is the Post Office's own set issued when it became a public corporation in 1969. To choose the highly complex subject of Post Office Technology as appropriate to the very restrictive nature of a stamp betrayed a lack of understanding of the limitations of the medium. It was far more the subject for a short film than a set of four stamps. The designer himself, David Gentleman, told me: 'The first step is to have a topic that people can respond to. You can scare people away by commemorating subjects that aren't worth commemorating or which look as though they are the result of pressures rather than a spontaneous choice.'

I can well remember all the arguments which were advanced at the time: 'We must be seen to be forward-looking; we must not look over our shoulder at our past, however glorious, for that would appear as though we were changing our status with some reluctance' even though in some respects that may have been true.

The reasoning at the time seemed logical enough, but the issue in the end did not proclaim the brave new world that the Post Office, in its new guise, would create. And it was not the designer's fault that it failed to be a very distinguished set.

Maybe, too, the same thing could be said about the BBC issue which commemorated 50 years of continuous daily radio broadcasting. Obviously the Post Office could not afford to ignore such a birthday, but there was built into the subject a well-nigh insurmountable problem. How can a designer give visual expression to what for the public has only been an auditory experience? However manfully David Gentleman battled with the problem, even he was not wholly satisfied with the result. This, of course, is typical of the dilemma in which the Post Office often finds itself, and in the end there is no alternative but to accept a mediocre result.

Even in the more recent issue of the Year of the Child, does a set of illustrations from children's books really start to get near to the world problem of deprived children as the United Nations sees it? And yet that was specific in the brief and it very nearly trivialized the whole sad subject.

Perhaps there were times when the Post Office tried too hard to appear to be liberal-minded and maybe went out of its way to listen too intently to specialized advice. It was then the habit to seek informed opinion from those organizations which were most involved in the particular subject of an issue, sometimes mistakenly referred to as the sponsors. And indeed the results of such consultations were, in the main, most valuable in helping the Post Office to define the brief. There were times, naturally, when the sponsors could only describe their problem in terms of the visual solution as they saw it, and in those circumstances it became essential to explain that design decisions were a matter for the Post Office. What it was seeking from them was guidance on attitudes.

With hindsight there is one recent issue where this collaboration did not in fact work, and that was on the occasion of the centenary of Graham Bell's telephone in 1976. It seemed perfectly natural that advice should be sought from the Telecommunications side of the Post Office as to how they would see this issue. After long discussions it was agreed that we should try to portray the sociological benefits of communication which only the telephone can bestow. A wholly reasonable brief until the designers tried to make it work. What was not fully appreciated was the inadequacy of the stamp as a medium for moralizing. The brief that had been developed was again more appropriate for a short documentary film, and although Philip Sharland produced some quite nice visual results, the message did not come across as clearly as it should have done. But that was not his fault.

Conversely the energy issue of 1978 does work, because there was no attempt to make a propaganda point. A similar brief to that for Graham Bell could have been developed for energy, with all the arguments about conservation, benefits from North Sea oil and the like, and it would have failed. Fortunately Peter Murdoch made a perfectly straightforward graphic statement with obvious success.

In many respects the Post Office is in an unenviable position on this question of subject choice and interpretation. By the very nature of its business, it imposes on the public certain conditions of choice which cannot be avoided and through its monopolistic state must inevitably deny its customers the opportunity to exercise personal choice on a very personal basis. If a customer doesn't like the look of the stamps he sees in the post office he cannot go next door and buy some other ones that he does like.

Up to a point the Post Office does accept that it has a responsibility, in democratic theory at least, to give the public what it wants, but at the same time it recognizes that such a responsibility can be fallacious. For just as the public is incapable of arriving at a representative point of view, even if it knew what it wanted, so the Post Office realizes that in the particular field of postal specialism it may know better. Certainly it has come to realize that it is rarely wise, as one Postmaster General would have had it believe, that it should aim 'to please the man on the Clapham Common bus.'

Ever since the publication of the first adhesive postage stamp, the Post Office has been very jealous of its responsibility to establish and maintain the highest standards of production, be they in the art, the design or the printing of its stamps. To that end it has always sought the advice of experts in fields related to the arts and sciences of stamp production, for it laid little claim to being skilled in matters of aesthetic judgement. As a result it set a standard of performance which few postal administrations have equalled. Over the years those standards have inevitably fluctuated, but due more to changing public taste than to Post Office inadequacy.

Today the Post Office is professionally in a stronger position to make up its own mind on matters of aesthetic judgement, having built into its permanent structure professional design skills. That these skills have not as yet been given adequate authority to function to the best of their ability is another matter, but by making itself self-sufficient in matters of design direction it has created its own dilemma, embarking at the same time on a very positive marketing policy which could very well be at odds with its traditional responsibility to maintain high standards of stamp design.

Not a very easy situation to resolve and indeed this dychotomy does have a very strong influence on the next contributory factor in stamp production – that of the designer.

2 Policy pressures on design

Design is not only as good as the skills and creative imagination of the designer can make it, it is as good as the client will allow it to be. In the stamp production programme, it is the Post Office who dictates the ultimate design quality of the stamp rather than the designer, for it has to decide first on the stylistic nature of the design it has in mind, before choosing who shall produce it. Does it see, for example, an illustrator's or a designer's solution? To a degree the subject itself will suggest the style, but the interpretation will reflect the taste of the Post Office as much as the skill of the designer or illustrator. Will the subject best be expressed in an abstract or symbolic manner, as with Peter Murdoch's EEC set, or in naturalistic way, say like Kristin Rosenberg's Roses or Marjorie Saynor's Explorers? But what dictated the difference between Andrew Restall's cycling stamp in his Commonwealth Games issue of 1970 and Fritz Wegner's Cycling set in 1978? Both, in their respective ways, are extremely good designers and illustrators, yet the decision to use the one or the other for virtually the same subject reflects very clearly Post Office attitudes at the time. In the end of course it is the designer's individual style that will determine the nature of the design, not necessarily its quality. For example, I would find it well nigh impossible to arrange, in order of merit, all the stamps that have been devoted to architecture. They all have their own individual qualities and the choice of the designer for a particular issue was made for what seemed to the Post Office at the time to be a good reason.

This problem of stylistic choice is made more difficult to solve when more than one designer is commissioned for the same issue, for in a way it betrays a certain indecision on the part of the Post Office. Then there are times, of course, when it is essential that a degree of choice is built into the submissions to the Palace, and indeed that has always been done where the issue has been personal to the Queen and her family; but unless alternative designs are sought for very well-defined and clearly understood reasons, then the exercise can only add confusion to an already difficult problem, as well as being rather expensive.

This is not a question to which there is only one answer: if the process of stamp production allows for decisions to be made on the basis of consensus of opinion drawn from more than one source, then the real benefit which can derive from personal and professional design direction will be eroded. And this continuing involvement between the Post Office and the designer, when conducted at a professional level, is at the heart of all design direction and can only suffer when the Post Office speaks with more than one voice.

The pressures put on that small area of professional design activity in Postal Headquarters are insistent and may not readily be ignored. But the temptation of permanent staff to regard the whole design game as being peripheral to their own particular specialism, be it operational or marketing, is great. And understandably so. Yet it is not easy to defend the argument that, when all is done, public appraisal of a stamp will be based on what it sees, and what the public does not see are the supposedly sound selling points and operational requirements which have been built into the design. For that is the way in which stamps are judged.

It was, of course, the liberalizing of Post Office stamp issuing policy in 1964 that created these problems, because the question of design standards applies more to pictorial issues where the dividing line between postage stamps and cigarette cards sometimes becomes very difficult to discern. And the reason, without doubt, is the urge to create a popular product. It is exactly on this issue that the Post Office is in danger of losing sight of its prime responsibility of maintaining the highest standard of stamp design.

Speaking at a Seminar held at the Philatelic Unit at Sussex University in September 1971, Brian Crowther, Head of Philatelic Marketing at the Post Office, had this to say: 'The principal factor in any marketing operation must be the product – the stamps which we issue. It must be recognized that commitment to philatelic marketing with increased profit as its aim implies acceptance of new disciplines in some aspects of stamp issuing policy. The subjects which I regard as most likely to capture the interest of collectors should be distinctively British, but attractive to enthusiasts in the philatelically significant areas of the world: Western Europe, North America, Japan, Australasia and South Africa. The treatment of the subject should be acceptable to the mass of collectors and designs should exploit any possible appeal to the growing thematic market.' No question here of what Crowther thought a good marketing stamp should be like and it is a point of view held just as firmly today by his successors, as it was in those early years of stamp marketing.

I asked Nigel Walmsley, the present Director of Postal Marketing, what his stamp issuing policy is:

'Our aim, which, I believe, we are usually successful in realizing, is to select subjects which will be generally recognized as fitting for depiction on stamps, by both the general public and the collector alike, and our own experience is that there is common ground here. As you know we have always welcomed ideas for subjects commended to us from all parts of the community. Our stance is to be as receptive and flexible as practical and to avoid "doctrinaire" pre-conceptions which might otherwise lead us to overlook novel opportunities.

2/1,2,3 Two of Peter
Murdoch's 1972 EEC stamps,
Kristin Rosenberg's Roses
(1976) and Marjorie Saynor's
Explorers (1972)

2/4 & 5 Cycling: Andrew
Restall's stamps of 1970 and
Fritz Wegner's of 1978

In making a final choice of subjects each year from the wealth of suggestions, we do have to have regard to those subjects which lend themselves best to good visual treatment and in making this judgement we do, of course, draw on expert advice.

As to design standards, we unhesitatingly aspire to the best. All our long experience confirms that the higher the quality of design the greater the degree of interest from all customers. One of the prime functions of the design adviser is, as you know, to seek out artists and designers capable of producing work of the highest quality within a wide range of individual styles. In this area the design adviser and the artists/designers are able to draw on the help of the Stamp Advisory Committee, which makes a vital contribution.'

On the other hand where there is a secondary reason for an issue, be it an event, a birthday or some other commemoration, it would seem reasonable to seek a solution which identifies the subject with an immediacy of recognition that leaves no doubt in the viewer's mind as to what the reason for the issue is. And to achieve this the designer does not have to resort to representational pictorialism, even though that is how the marketing pundits would like it.

It is not so long ago that the whole idea of pictorial stamps was anathema, not only to the Post Office, but to its artists and supporters. Certainly this objection, strongly held by the monarch, explains why no pictorial stamps were issued during the reign of George V with the exception of the Wembley issue of 1924 and the Postal Union Congress of 1929 (see p. 41). For the Post Office to issue a set of stamps on dogs or to commission a well-known cartoonist to commemorate the 200th birthday of The Derby was then unthinkable, and up to a point I would agree.

In *The Times*, in September 1936, Eric Gill propounded his own philosophy on stamp design. 'A postage stamp,' he wrote, 'is primarily a symbolic device, not a picture. The business of making stamps is about as far removed from the studio as can be and the job of the designer is a strictly functional one.'

Writing a year later to A. Tydeman, Controller of the Post Office Supplies Department, Gill commented: 'From my point of view the whole idea of a picture stamp is unreasonable . . . It seems to me that to use a pictorial subject is simply to pander to sentimentality and the appetite of collectors of something curious.' Some years later, writing in *The Listener* in February 1944 Edmund Dulac stated quite clearly his own views on what makes a good stamp:

2/6 & 7 One of the three Red Cross Centenary stamps of 1963: immediate graphic identification of the message; and two stamps from the Metropolitan Police issue of 1979: the pictorial representation of the message

2/8 & 9 Gill's stamp
celebrating the centenary of
the First Adhesive Postage
Stamp and Dulac's Festival of
Britain

'Like a label, a stamp must be clear and easy to read, it must convey all
the information it is destined to convey: country of origin, value and the
word meaning postage . . . Other considerations, however, soon in-
tervene as reasons for putting more on a stamp than simple lettering and
figures. One is the fear of forgery which in the early days led to an
elaboration of engraving devices that often produced very attractive
results. Another is nothing less than a desire to advertise, to call attention
to the good position of a nation in the world by displaying portraits of its
ruler or its great men, views of the land or pictures of its history and
commercial activities.

It is only when the label becomes a picture that stamp design de-
generates. This does not mean that good design is altogether incom-
patible with the picture notion of a stamp; excellent results can be
achieved when stamp designing is considered the business of an artist.

A good artist is an invaluable asset. I mean by this a man who
combines good drawing with a sense of pattern; and by pattern I mean
an arrangement of patches of black and white, preferably on simple
lines, that in itself will give pleasure to the eye and is made up of elements
so broadly treated or so simplified that the idea to be conveyed stands
out clearly.'

An admirable description of what today is called a designer.

True, both Gill and Dulac were writing about the permanent issues
more than about commemorative stamps. But both were involved later
with issues for specific occasions, Gill by providing the lettering for the
centenary of the First Adhesive Postage Stamps in 1940 and Dulac for the
2½d Festival of Britain value in 1951. In both instances they remained
faithful to their proclaimed beliefs and resisted any temptation to be
pictorial. How they would have reacted to today's stamp issuing policies is
impossible to judge, but in so far as between them they managed – in spite
of their differences – to produce one of the best definitive issues ever to
come out of the Post Office, that of George VI in 1937, makes me think
they would have been a formidable match against any attempt to lower
their very high standards.

On 20 October 1953 Viscount Elibank, in the House of Lords, had
raised the matter of the possible issue of small low-value pictorial stamps
portraying some of the scenic beauties or historic monuments of the British
Isles, in order to attract tourists. Replying for the Government Lord
Selkirk said: 'The low value stamps, that is stamps up to a value of 1s 6d in
their present size, do not lend themselves to effective pictorial designs.'

Putting the same question a year later, Lord Elibank had much the same reply from the PMG himself, Lord de la Warr. Undeterred, the noble lord repeated his question four months later, to which the PMG again replied: 'I must confess that my experience of these stamps has shown how difficult it is to combine well the head of the Queen with good pictorial designs.' It is interesting that throughout all the discussion it was never suggested that the Queen's head should be left off to make the design easier. Quite the contrary, it was stressed that her effigy must remain.

The following year Stanley Gibbons were approached by Lord Macpherson, who had been supporting Lord Elibank in his campaign, and later by Lord Elibank himself, to ascertain their philatelic judgement on the matter. Although they admitted to holding the view that small pictorial stamps were not a practical proposition, they nevertheless were in support of the purpose of the stamps, as an aid to tourism. As a result Mr C. P. Rang, the editor of *Gibbons Stamp Monthly*, designed a set of seven stamps. When, therefore, on May 17 1956 Lord Elibank yet again moved a debate on the same subject he was able to exhibit proofs of the proposed new stamps. In spite of the fact that the PMG was reported as being by no means unsympathetic to the idea, nothing seems to have happened beyond the possible inclusion of a pictorial stamp on air letter forms. It is questionable whether these very undistinguished stamps did the cause any good.

In 1965, however, Stanley Gibbons again returned to the fray and commissioned a professional designer, Jock Kinneir FSIA, to design a new set of twelve small pictorials. Harrisons printed them in photogravure as a miniature sheet, which was given away with copies of *Stamp Monthly*. Under the heading 'Gibbons want British Stamps to Tell the World about Britain', the stamps, and the idea behind them, were given extensive coverage, but once again the scheme fell upon deaf Post Office ears and fortunately nothing more was heard of it.

This experiment demonstrated the wisdom of getting a good designer to cope with even a bad subject, for even if one regards the whole idea of small pictorials as an impracticable one, Jock Kinneir's designs are so much more professional than the earlier Gibbons efforts.

So dogmatic, even passionate, was the insistence by artists and designers of a generation ago that a stamp was not a picture, that I could not resist the temptation to see how graphic designers today felt about this question, accepting the fact that the recent spate of pictorial issues may have influenced their judgement.

I therefore went to three eminent designers who have designed stamps and who between them have accounted for a formidable number of issues.

2/10 The 1937 George VI definitives by Gill and Dulac

2/11 & 12 Two of the landscape stamps designed by C. P. Rang in 1955 and Jock Kinneir's version of 1965

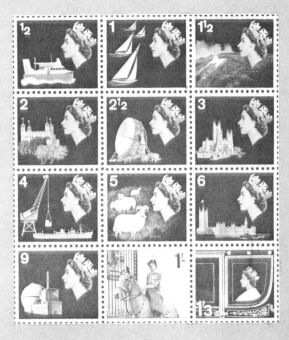

I put the question first to Jeffery Matthews.

SR: 'At the time of the one and only Edward VIII definitive stamp, there raged in the correspondence columns of the Press a great argument as to whether a stamp was a label or a picture. What is your view, today?'

JM: 'I tend to err on the side of regarding a stamp more as a label than a picture. Many issues recently – and I'm not speaking only of British Commemoratives – have become too much like little pictures. I'm not saying that they may not be collectable, but that's another question.

I'm rather traditionalist in my view and my background. I'm slightly stuffy about this question. Since Britain was the first country to produce an adhesive stamp, I believe we should have some respect for that heritage and that whatever pressures are put upon us we should have some regard for the past and show a little dignity about the fact that we are the only nation that doesn't have to put our name on the stamp. Because we are identified by the sovereign's effigy on the label it should always play an important part in the design. There is a tendency in some commemorative issues for the Queen's head and the value to be regarded as unnecessary evils which have to be put up with. I baulk at that straight away; maybe that is my traditionalist background again. In my view, a British stamp should have the Queen's head and the value, and everything else should be secondary to that. Perhaps that precludes the idea of the little picture.'

I then put the same question to David Gentleman, explaining what had prompted my enquiry.

SR: 'I've been talking to Jeffery Matthews on this question of whether a stamp is a label or a picture. Where does your heart lie in this particular argument?'

DG: 'I think that labels are appropriate for long-term definitives, but I do not believe that you can prevent commemoratives from being illustrative because in any other approach you would very quickly run out of the available language and motifs. To me pictures are an essential component of commemoratives.'

SR: 'It is interesting to compare the earlier commemoratives of the reign where the label concept was very strongly held. The dictated size of the Wilding head inevitably dominated the design, so that the subject was of secondary importance. Was that a wise condition for the Post Office to make?'

DG: 'Yes, I'm sure it was, for as soon as you try to put anything else on a stamp other than simply framing the head, there is bound to be a tug-of-war between the two elements unless the head is treated purely as a typographic one. This has only become possible with the flat silhouette instead of the three-quarter realistic view.'

SR: 'I suppose it is reasonable to assume that pictorial stamps are popular. Do you see, though, a risk of killing the goose, as it were?'

DG: 'I think it's important that stamps should not become like cigarette cards, with each one a pretty picture. They should be more significant than that. The pictorial content is admirable, but it needs to be very carefully organized within the space and well and tightly designed. I really believe that the whole process of designing is reconciling and organizing a lot of very complicated elements within a small area, without the result looking as if there had been any problem. That's what's difficult.'

And lastly I approached Philip Sharland on a rather broader base.

SR: 'When I wrote to you the other day, you sent back a comment, which I liked, to the effect that you didn't think there was much you could say about contemporary stamps because nowadays the Post Office was leaning so heavily on illustrative and pictorial stamps that you felt the designer had almost become an anachronism. Were you really serious about that?'

PS: 'Yes.'

SR: 'We're back to the old argument again of the picture versus the label. Do you feel that maybe the Post Office has overplayed the picture game?'

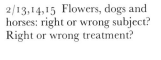

2/13,14,15 Flowers, dogs and horses: right or wrong subject? Right or wrong treatment?

PS: 'They have as far as "designers" are concerned. The real stamp designers, people like David Gentleman – who always provides ingenious, inventive solutions, whether you like them or not, and always impeccably done – are being passed over in favour of a maxi-market philosophy which aims at diagnosing what is most likely to sell to the widest public. Flowers, dogs, horses, birds in perpetuity, I suppose.'

SR: 'But do you attribute this to the wrong choice of subject or the wrong choice of designer or illustrator?'

PS: 'Well, a bit of both I'm afraid. It's the right sort of subject for people who draw flowers and horses. It may be the right sort of subject for maximum sales, it's not the right sort of subject for people who have, over the past ten or fifteen years, been doing stamps that I would find more graphically interesting: I'm not really turned on by a well-rendered stallion nor a nicely-painted rose. Illustrators quite often seem to have difficulty in arranging their material in what I would call an attractive and exciting way.'

Miniaturist design demands a quite specific approach, being much more than an ability to paint in such a small area. If we accept that a designer, to be any good at all, must possess a high degree of painterly skills and craftsmanship, it is his ability to analyse the subject and extract from it the one meaningful factor which becomes the sole element in his design. For stamp design is an intellectual process demanding a capacity to crystallize a problem into an inevitable graphic expression, before it is an ability to paint a picture. Admittedly to possess that ability is undoubtedly an advantage, but unless it is supported by an equal ability to design, then the result may well be only a picture, lacking that elusive quality of synthesis which is the essential mark of good design.

3 It all began with the Penny Black

One of the many bright ideas which emerged, remotely, as a result of the Reform Bill of 1832 was the adhesive postage stamp, and in particular the Penny Black. Attracted by the attacks made in Parliament by Robert Wallace, MP for Greenock, on the inefficiency of the Post Office, Rowland Hill published his pamphlet *Post Office Reform, Its Importance and Practicability* in which he set out his argument condemning the high cost, inefficiency and privileged abuse of the Postal service. The reform he advocated relied on a uniform postal rate of 1d for a letter weighing $\frac{1}{2}$ ounce for delivery anywhere in the United Kingdom, the charge to be levied when the letter was posted, instead of when it was delivered, which was the current practice.

Almost as an afterthought Hill had suggested that if every house was fitted with a letter box and postage was pre-paid 'the letter carrier would drop the letters and, having knocked, he would pass on as fast as he could walk.' The system Rowland Hill sought to reform was then a cash-on-delivery one, and time wasted in awaiting an answer at a house, argument with the recipient over payment, often repeated visits to get an answer, resulted inevitably in a very heavy financial loss for the Post Office.

It was therefore this new proposal for the pre-payment of a postal service which brought about the production of a receipt or label, as it was first called.

Ultimately Rowland Hill's recommendations for reform of the Post Office were accepted, and in September 1839 the Lords of the Treasury sent out invitations to artists, scientists and the public for the submission of ideas and designs in connection with the introduction of prepaid post and the penny post.

Some five weeks were allowed for the competition, yet more than two and a half thousand submissions were received: under 50 of them had anything to do with an adhesive stamp and of them only four were considered to justify an award.

Before the competition was launched, Rowland Hill had described his own idea for a stamp as being 'a bit of paper just large enough to bear the stamp (that is the cancellation) and covered at the back with a glutinous wash which the user might, by applying a little moisture, attach to the back of the letter.' It should be remembered that Rowland Hill's stamp assumed the continuation of the then current practice by which a letter sheet, when folded and sealed on the back, made its own cover, without an envelope.

There can be no doubt that the over-riding concern in the design of this new label was security against fraudulent copy and re-use, and not surprisingly for in those days a 1d stamp was a valuable commodity.

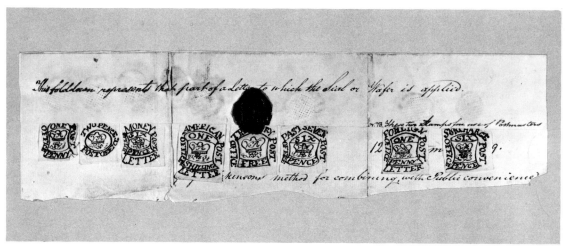

3/1,2 The engraved design
submitted by C. F. Whiting and
the drawings produced by
G. Dickinson

One of the four winners of the competition, Benjamin Cheverton, made an interesting point on this question of security when he wrote: 'Now it so happens that the eye being educated to the perception of differences in the features of the face, the detection of any deviation in the forgery would be more easy – the difference of effect would strike an observer more readily than in the case of letters or any mere mechanical or ornamental device, although he may be unable perhaps to point out where the differences lies or in what it consists.' And what more familiar portrait than that of the beloved Queen! Cheverton also recommended that the stamps should be printed on rolls of watermarked security paper.

The competition acted as a great stimulus to inventive thinking and although the great majority of entries were of little value, those of the winners are worth recording.

Perhaps the most decorative was the engraved design submitted by Charles Fenton Whiting which was printed in two colours simultaneously from a combined set of dies. His obsession with the security aspect of his design was typical of many entries, but the strong emphasis he placed on the numeral value is significant. George Dickinson, the paper maker, sent in some hand-drawn designs for what were in fact labels denoting different services and at the same time he suggested that they should be printed in sheets on special security watermarked paper.

James Chalmers, a bookseller and printer in Dundee, submitted a number of essays of a circular design and cancelled with the word 'used' and proposed a 'Post Office town stamp'. Chalmers had been a strong advocate of postal reform for a number of years and as early as 1834 was experimenting with printing identical designs onto sheets of gummed paper. In February 1838 he sent a long memorandum to Robert Wallace, MP, setting out his proposals for implementing Rowland Hill's plan for a uniform rate of postage by the use of adhesive stamps rather than stamped envelopes or letter sheets.

With the memorandum Chalmers also sent designs for his adhesive stamp, one of which is cancelled with a Dundee date-stamp. It was these early proposals which were later to lead to a bitter controversy between Patrick Chalmers, his son, and Rowland Hill's son Pearson, each claiming for their respective fathers public recognition for the invention of the adhesive stamp.

Ultimately, however, Rowland Hill sought the advice of three Royal Academicians recommended by the President of the Academy, one of whom was William Wyon, who some years earlier had engraved the bas-relief portrait of the young Queen to be struck on a medal commemorating

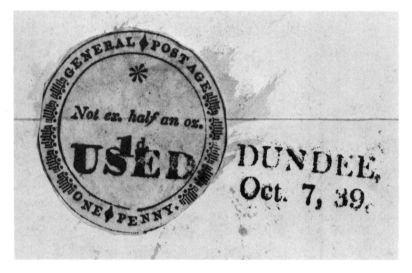

3/3 The circular design
submitted by J. Chalmers

her first visit to the City of London in 1837. In the same year Henry
Corbould, FSA, had been working on some portraits of the Queen commis-
sioned by the security printers, Perkins Bacon & Petch, possibly using
Wyon's head as a model, and it was from these drawings that Charles and
Frederick Heath ultimately made the engraving for the portrait on the
Penny Black.

The Heaths produced a number of engravings of the head all on
backgrounds which had been machine-engraved by a process currently in
use on bank notes, as a further safeguard against forgery.

What makes the design and production of the first adhesive stamp so
fascinating today is the insistence on the wholly functional nature of the
product; a typical industrial design problem. And although the result was
one of the most beautiful stamps we have ever produced, the prime concern
was not to create a thing of beauty. Rowland Hill himself had once
volunteered that 'labels, if made of some paper difficult to imitate and, like
the medicine stamps, printed from complex plates with various colours in
the same impression, thus requiring the ingenuity of the paper-maker, the
engraver and the printer, would be secure against forgery.'

It is, of course, the quality of the engraving which makes the stamp so
lovely to look at and the concept of a light image against a dark background gives it a brilliancy which is almost dazzling.

But alas, the Penny Black was technically too good. The engravers had insisted, quite rightly, that such an engraving could only properly be printed in black, but the ink that they used was far too permanent to prevent the red cancellation from being removed, with the help of a solvent. So that after only a year's life the Penny Black became the Penny Red and so lost much of its original beauty.

Over the next forty years, new values were added to the range and with the exception of the twopenny blue, all were of a different design. It is surprising that, after the brilliant success of the first stamp, none that followed really matched it in design. Admittedly one or two of the later values are quite pretty, notably the fourpenny red of 1855 and the one shilling green of 1867, but generally the design is pedestrian, as though the spark had gone out of the Post Office and its printers.

Certainly by 1883 United Kingdom stamp design had reached such a low ebb, in terms of sheer functional inefficiency, that neither the public nor the Post Office staff could stand it any longer and the resulting outcry forced the Government to set up a Committee to enquire into the whole question of postage stamp design.

The terms of reference for the Committee make very interesting reading, for again they stress the need for efficiency and security from forgery and re-use, in fact an excellent industrial design brief.

3/4a The Wyon medal, and
3/4b Henry Corbould's drawing

3/5 The portrait on the Penny Black

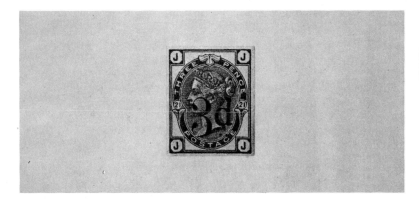

3/6 One of the De La Rue large numeral essays submitted in 1882

'1. It is of the first importance that, in any scheme of Postage stamps which may be devised, there should be such a variety of colour, form and design as to render the stamps of different values easily distinguishable from one another, both by the Post Office officials and by the public, not only when first used, but also after they have been cancelled.

2. The stamps should be printed in so thorough and effective a manner as to prevent fraudulent use of them after they have once passed through the Post.

3. They should also be such in manufacture and design as to preclude the possibility of imitation.

4. Regard should be had to the desirableness of providing stamps which shall have as much artistic merit as is compatible with the first three conditions.

5. The whole subject requires very careful and deliberate consideration, with the help of information and suggestion, not only from practical officers of the Department who may be called to assist the Committee, but also from any persons, skilful in design or otherwise, of whose knowledge and taste the Committee may desire to avail themselves; for it has become most desirable, in the light of previous failures, that an amended scheme should now be devised which may hold out every reasonable promise of efficiency and permanence.'

Whoever it was who drafted these instructions had an understanding of the factors which govern the 'design' of stamps, which was quite impressive for his period.

3/7 The 'different shapes' proposal re-emerging in 1884: the number of sides relates to the numeral and the shape and size of the stamp is consistent

3/8 De La Rue's schemes
relying on the large numeral

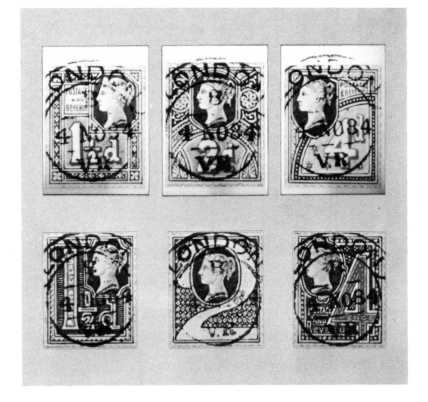

3/9 The gigantic numeral:
confusion and illegibility

But if the Committee's terms of reference were remarkable, the resulting designs which were submitted for its consideration were even more so.

In 1882, before the Committee was set up, the printers De La Rue had submitted to the Board of Inland Revenue a set of essays of each value, printed in lilac with a large numeral overprint in black of the value, foreshadowing later proposals which used even larger numerals.

The previous year Mr T. Jeffrey, Controller of the London Postal Service, who was later to become Chairman of the 1884 Stamp Committee, had submitted to the Board a scheme based on individual shapes of stamps to identify different values. An ingenious if somewhat impractical proposal, but one which was to re-emerge three years later from Mr Adams, a clerk in the office of the Controller, who had adapted the scheme by making the varying sided shapes of the design relate to the monetary value, but all to be printed on a stamp of constant shape and size.

Two more schemes were produced by De la Rue, both of them relying heavily on the large value numeral.

G. R. Smith, Controller of the Returned Letter Office tried to reinforce the value numeral by underprinting a comparable number of horizontal bars. A reasonable theory, but which in practice tends more to confuse than to clarify.

None of the proposals was quite so adventurous as the very large numeral scheme, which, with a little more design care and attention, could have had some of the confusion worked out of the pattern, which became well-nigh illegible after cancellation.

In many respects the Jubilee issue, which resulted from the Committee's deliberations, was a disappointment. It was decidedly an improvement on those it superseded, especially in some of the two-colour combinations,

many of which are quite lovely. But in keeping rigidly to the first term of
reference, which is quite categoric in demanding that 'there should be such
a variety of colour, form and design', the Committee robbed the issue of
any sense of formality. There were in fact twelve wholly different designs,
the only common element being the Sovereign's effigy.

But if this issue brought a certain stability to the postal service, it also
established the pattern of stamp design for the next forty years, a pattern
which, in the relatively short time since the appearance of the Penny Black,
had changed so radically. Gone was the original directness of statement
and simplicity of design. True, with greater values being included in the
range and the increased emphasis that consequently had to be placed on
the value numeral, the Queen's head could no longer command the
dominant place it originally held. It was not until 1967 that Arnold
Machin, with his definitive stamps, replaced some of the dignity and
authority that was lost in the Jubilee issue.

The design idiom in this issue was so strongly held that even a change of
reign in 1901 was not regarded as sufficient justification for a radical
change in design, and poor Edward VII had to be content with having his
own portrait slotted into the space recently vacated by his mother. Of the
eleven low-values issued in 1902, eight are identical in all other respects to
those issued in 1887. Maybe there was some sense in retaining the basic
visual identification for the majority of values, but it seemed to herald the
long period of conservatism that overshadowed stamp design and production for the next thirty-five years.

It is tempting to look for some sociological influence which not only
made Edward VII stamps so fundamentally Victorian, but also made
George V issues decidedly not. The formula was of course the same; the
monarch's effigy surrounded by decoration appropriate to the period. But
whereas the decoration in the Victorian issues had a design quality of its
own, that in George V and in some values of Edward VII ($\frac{1}{2}$d, $2\frac{1}{2}$d and 7d)
was beginning to show signs of debasement.

Certainly the 1913–18 Seahorse high values have a quality about their
production which is remarkable (see p. 12), as indeed do the Wembley
Exhibition issues of 1924 and 1925, but they are very much in the same
stylistic mode of the current definitives.

The first quarter of the century were overall dull years: nothing relieved
the visual boredom of the stamps until we get to the Universal Postal
Union Congress issue of 1929 (see p. 41).

It was John Farleigh who made the first break with traditional dec-
oration in his two stamps for this issue. His $\frac{1}{2}$d and $2\frac{1}{2}$d are a determined

3/10 The design produced for
Queen Victoria's 1887 issue
and how Edward VII had to
put up with it

attempt to try to reflect the design idiom of the period and they mark a
turning point away from the rather duller stamps of the early part of the
reign. Nelson's £1, rather naturally, was in the manner of his Wembley
Exhibition designs of five years earlier and mixes uncomfortably with
Farleigh's more direct and simplified approach, skilled as it is as an engraving. It has always seemed odd to me that, to celebrate a Congress dedicated
to harmony amongst international postal administrations, the United
Kingdom should show herself in the shape of St George slaying the dragon
at her gate. Hardly a welcoming gesture to her foreign postal guests!

But it is, I believe, the Barnett Freedman Silver Jubilee set of 1935 that
should properly be regarded as being the initiator of a wholly new ap-

3/11,12 George V definitive
(above) and some Edward VII
values: decadence of decoration

proach to stamp design. Fortunately the Post Office had sought the advice of Sir Stephen Tallents, the first Public Relations Officer at the GPO, and Mr Kenneth Clark, then Director of the National Gallery, who found no difficulty in selecting out of twenty designs one by Barnett Freedman. Certainly none of the other designs came anywhere near his well-controlled set, which brilliantly exploited the photogravure process. Remarkable as his designs were, perhaps equally remarkable was the courage and imagination of the Post Office to publish them (see p. 42).

If Barnett Freedman's designs had been welcomed, admittedly more by the professionals than by the public, as revolutionary in a benevolent sort of way, the issue that followed a year later in 1936, the Accession issue of Edward VIII, was seen as being positively anarchic. Never had an issue generated so much heated correspondence in the Press both for and against the stamp. Everyone seemed to join in the melée – artists, designers and the public at large. What sparked off the trouble was a rather unwise statement by the Post Office, made at the time of issue, that no artists had been commissioned to submit designs, but instead the printers, Harrison & Sons, had been asked to prepare designs in their own studios. In addition, suggestions for the stamp had been received by the Post Office from philatelists, one of whom was a young member of the Torquay and Exeter Philatelic Societies, Mr H. J. Brown. Harrisons were also asked to develop these designs. Ultimately a modification of Mr Brown's submission was approved by the King and subsequently issued.

Today Mr Brown, though still modest, is none the less very entertaining in his recollection of the affair. He was 'swotting' at home for his actuarial exams, having just left Monkton Combe School in 1935, and was impressed by an article in *Gibbons Stamp Monthly*, to which he subscribed, which criticised the current designs of the George V definitives. Having firm ideas of his own on stamps, and considering the imminent need for fresh designs for the new reign, he started to put his ideas on paper. With his father's encouragement, he wrote to the GPO asking permission to submit his proposals. The letter he received from the Postal Services Department in reply speaks for itself:

'Sir: I am directed by the Postmaster General to refer to your letter of the 13th of February, and to say that there is no objection to your submitting a design for the new issue of postage stamps. I should perhaps mention, however, that the design is usually chosen from the competitive designs of distinguished artists. I am, Sir, Your obedient Servant.'

In due course, therefore, a highly finished 3b pencil drawing, ten times

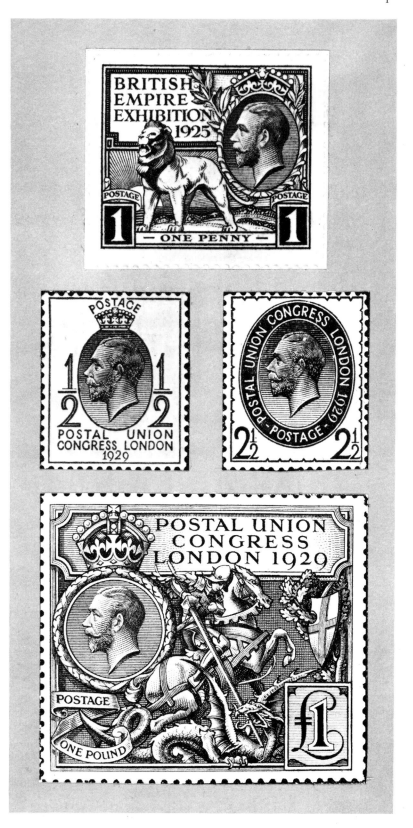

3/13,14,15 The Wembley
Exhibition issue of 1924–25,
John Farleigh's Universal Postal
Union stamps of 1929, and
Nelson's £1 stamp for the same
issue

3/16 One of the stamps from
the 1935 Silver Jubilee issue

stamp size, was carefully packed in a dress-box and despatched to the
GPO, with Brown full of apprehension lest anyone should smudge the
highly vulnerable work – for at that time he had not heard of fixative.

Nothing happened and he heard no more until Tuesday, 1 September
1936, the day that the stamps were issued, when this letter (dated 26
August) was received at the Brown home:

'Sir: I am directed by the Postmaster General to refer to your letter of the
4th of April, with which you enclosed a drawing for a suggested postage
stamp of the new reign.

The design was not considered suitable for adoption as it stood, but it
appeared to present certain suggestions which, although they were not
novel, might be successfully developed in designing a stamp for printing
by the photogravure process. It was therefore shewn to Messrs Harrison
& Sons, who hold the contract for the supply of postage stamps and who
were engaged at the time in the preparation of designs for consideration.

Stamps of the new reign will appear shortly, and you will see that the
design which has been selected bears some features in common with that
which you suggested.

The Postmaster General desires me to express his warm appreciation
of the interest which you have taken in this matter.

I am, Sir, Your obedient Servant.'

3/17,18 Edward VIII definitive
of 1936 and H. J. Brown's
drawing submitted for the 1936
definitives

There is every evidence that the GPO had become highly embarrassed by the whole affair, the more so when Mr Brown senior hinted that its behaviour towards his son had been somewhat mean, to say the least. A marginal note, in a GPO hand, on that letter states 'the best course is to lie low and say nothing.'

But if the GPO wanted to lie doggo, so did young Brown – deriving some enjoyment from the furious press correspondence which the issue had generated. But not so his uncle, Mr Wilson Brown, who in fairness to his nephew, 'spilled the beans', as he said. In January 1937 *Gibbons Stamp Monthly* told the whole story and reproduced Hubert Brown's design alongside the issued stamp, demonstrating exactly the extent to which 'the design which has been selected bears some features in common with that which you suggested', as the GPO put it.

Thereafter the story became a nine days wonder in the Press, with poor young Brown being pursued by a reporter from the *Daily Sketch* to the offices of a well-known insurance company, on the first day of his new job.

Meanwhile, the storm was raging in the press columns.

In a letter to *The Times* of 24 September 1936 Milner Gray, then Secretary of the young Society of Industrial Artists, wrote: 'There are in this country industrial artists practised in this branch of design, the distinction of whose work assures us that they are able to produce for our stamps designs which might well give a lead to the nations of the world. The names of these, in common with those of our leading authorities in other fields, are well enough known . . . In a matter of such relative national importance it would seem reasonable that, after a very careful investigation of the potential talent available, a short list of the best designers should be asked to submit designs for final selection by a Committee elected from those most competent to judge.' It was not until 1947 that Milner Gray's proposal was implemented by the setting up of a Stamp Advisory Panel by the Council of Industrial Design.

Surprisingly *The Times* itself had published, ten days earlier, a leader which had a rather patronising air about it: 'The new postage stamps have been well received, though correspondence in these columns shows that satisfaction is not universal.

Not much attention need be paid at this stage to criticisms of details, such as the spacing of the elements or the style of the lettering, nor is it much to the point to talk at large about art and artists. There are many artists, eminent in their own field, who are quite incapable of designing a good postage stamp.

The first thing to get right in a work of this kind is content; and there is general satisfaction that the country has been given a stamp which explains its purpose without irrelevant verbal detail and otiose ornament.

The most important consideration is the process of printing . . . The new Edwardian stamps introduce a portrait of the Sovereign which, selected with the photogravure process in view, is in complete consistency with it.'

From William Rothenstein on 15 September: 'You say that there are many artists eminent in their own field who are quite incapable of designing a good postage stamp. True; but is this the point? If there be but one should not his services be used? If no artist today can be trusted to design a decent postage stamp, let the Government at least be honest in the economy and shut up our schools of art, our national galleries and museums, these costly institutions having, in their eyes, proved useless.'

Harold Speed, the sculptor, writing angrily: 'You tell us that the Press have seen it and approved, and now public opinion is asked for. Why does England hold its artists in such contempt? Why are the Press and the public thought to be the proper authorities in matters of taste?'

On 23 September Eric Gill joined in: 'I should like, if you will allow me, to record my opinion that the new postage stamps of King Edward VIII are exceedingly good both in themselves as postage stamps and in facture . . . the new postage stamps are eminently an improvement on previous issues and mark a bold step in the right direction. The photograph is obviously a good photograph and its reproduction is an admirable example of mechanical expertise. The lettering, though not actually as good as plain lettering can be, is the right kind. The little Victorian crown fulfils its object of marking the fact that the stamp has Government authority. There is no unnecessary and consequently meaningless ornament. The only reasonable criticisms . . . are that it would have been possible, by a different lighting of the head of the King, to have avoided the gradated background . . . and the consequent outlining of the right-hand letters; it would have been possible to draw a better crown . . . and it would have been possible to design a better A and E. Above all it is a pity that the head of the King is cut off at the neck in the manner of a sculptured relief (with a sham shadow underneath the cut) thus destroying the integrity of the design. But these criticisms are all concerned with matters of secondary importance and should do nothing to prevent us from tendering to the Post Office the congratulations it deserves for releasing us from the banalities of imitation hand-engraving and stupid ornamentation.'

It was that last sentence that got Gill into such trouble, mainly from his fellow artists.

Edmund Dulac in *The Times* of 24 September 1936: 'The arguments in the controversy over the new postage stamps are becoming rather confused. The excellence of the reproduction, the absence of "meaningless" ornament, the unprecedented sales are offered as causes for congratulation. These debatable qualities have led people away from the main point. The only question of importance is whether, in the opinion of those who ought to know, the design is good or bad. One is therefore surprised to find such an authority as Mr Eric Gill adding further to the confusion.

The new stamps by their simplicity may, in principle, be an improvement on the old ones, but in principle only. One can argue that the elements chosen, King's head, crown, denomination, and lettering, are sufficient. An egg, some oil, vinegar, salt and pepper are sufficient elements for an excellent mayonnaise in the hands of a good cook. In the hands of a bad one they can be a mess.

This is the case with the present design. An artist – not necessarily a painter, but a designer with a sense of tone values and proportions – might have made of it an attractive pattern. As it stands Mr Gill's own criticisms should be thus amplified: the head is not good. Due, no doubt, to inefficient retouching, the hair is too dark, the likeness unfamiliar – many Press snapshots are infinitely better. The shadow under the short neck is, with a realistic head, almost gruesome; the shaded background is cheap-looking; the crown hardly recognisable as such; the lettering is commonplace and the composition ill-balanced and empty. The only good piece of designing is in the watermark.

Mr Gill says that these things are matters of secondary importance. If, in a fit of absent-mindedness, he had produced such a design, would he, on coming to his senses, consent to have his name put to it?'

Charles Wheeler, the sculptor, had much the same thing to say: 'After Mr Gill rightly praises the method of reproduction of the new issue of stamps as being in harmony with the age, he also rightly criticises the portrait, lettering and crown, and background, leaving only the numerals untouched. But "these criticisms" he says, "are all concerned with matters of secondary importance."

'Would Mr Gill tell us which are matters of primary importance? Is not "design" one and is that not conspicuously absent from the new stamps?'

Strong words. And that was not the end. The correspondence continued for another few weeks but more on questions of functionalism, machine production and good design. Inevitably it proved nothing.

There were some prophetic words, too, from Frank Pick of London Transport: 'Are the parts related together? Has the 1d any connection with postage? No. Has the crown any connection with the head? No. It is even a crown receding and not approaching, as it happens. Anticipating the Coronation, the 1d and the crown might well have changed places and what of design there is would still remain.'

It is easy to disagree with Eric Gill's somewhat off-hand dismissal of the apparent lack of concern for the minutiae of design and to resent a similar attitude in *The Times* leader, but in one thing Gill was assuredly right – that the new stamp pointed in the right direction and that from that moment onwards stamp design could only improve. Not that his pious hope was readily attainable and indeed there were lapses back into the old Edwardian mould. But by and large the Edward VIII stamp was a catalyst in so far as it brought the public and the professionals up short and made them re-appraise standards of acceptance that had become somewhat dulled.

What is so regrettable now, admittedly with a deal of hindsight, is that there was no-one in the Post Office or at Harrison's who appears to have been able to take Brown's extremely imaginative idea and turn it into a professional design.

It was so very nearly right, yet nobody held out a hand to this brave young man to help him over the hurdle that separates amateur from professional – as we did 35 years later with the Caxton issue.

If that had been done, maybe much of the criticism of his stamp, which in some respects was justified, could have been turned to praise and he would have been given credit – as was his due – for some very creative thinking. Perhaps this will go some way to make amends.

It is ironic that after such a public display of fisticuffs Gill and Dulac should find themselves working together the following year on the definitives for the new reign; also, they had both been invited to submit designs for the single stamp George VI Coronation issue. It was Dulac's design which was ultimately issued.

This stamp came in for a good deal of rather unfair criticism with *The Times* in its leader dubbing it a great disappointment. 'The stamp designed to mark an occasion so august as well as joyful, the first stamp in Great Britain to include the head of a Queen Consort should have made better use both of its opportunity and of its unusually attractive material. But with the best will in the world it is not possible to see in it any singleness of design. The crown and monogram divide, not join, the two heads. The patterns in the margins are meagre, and the whole too closely suggests the sort of thing a hospital issues for the charitable to stick on the backs of their letters.'

3/19,20 George VI
Coronation and two designs
from the definitive issue

A harsh judgement not wholly justified, for Dulac was trying to bridge
the gap between the rather elaborate ornament of the George V issues and
the somewhat bare simplicity of Edward VIII. His views on the use of
ornament in stamps had been very clearly stated the previous year in the
columns of that same august paper that was now taking him to task.

It was however rather more kind to the Gill/Dulac definitives. 'Mr Eric
Gill's lettering is aristocratic and distinguished – a great improvement on
the former sans-serif lettering; but the words also look too large for the
space. Mr Dulac's portrait of King George is admirable, and since the
background is plain, not shaded, there is no suggestion of the spotlight or
the cinema studio about it. The field is too full, and hence the general
impression is lacking in dignity.' But that is exactly what it did not lack,
being perhaps the most dignified low value stamp to have appeared for
many a long day. But it was perhaps his high value 2s 6d and 5s designs,

which were issued two years later, that made this Dulac set so memorable in spite of Somerset Herald's rather over-elaborated 10s and £1.

There is an uncanny fin-de-siècle feeling about these mid-reign issues, for after the very tightly controlled, almost austere issue for the Centenary of the First Adhesive Postage Stamp in 1940, British stamps were never to look the same again.

The years between 1939 and 1945 had changed fundamentally everyone's recollection and judgement of the immediate pre-war period, and although, for designers, the new thinking did not begin to blossom until the new Queen came to the throne in 1952, the later years of her father's reign were beginning to influence the next quarter century of stamp design and production.

4 The GPO and the COID

Perhaps one of the most significant events which was to have a quite dramatic effect on British stamp design and production was the setting up in 1944 of the Council of Industrial Design. Here at last was an authoritative Government body which would bring a new sense of professionalism to industrial design and would harness the growing involvement of this young profession.

As far as the Post Office is concerned it was ultimately to lead to a greater awareness of the need for it to be far more professional in its approach to design matters and to provide itself with the informed skills which are essential to efficient and worthwhile design direction.

In the matter of postage stamps, the Post Office had always been willing to seek outside help and advice in an area in which it did not regard itself as being professionally competent. Even in 1839, after the failure of the Treasury Competition to find an acceptable solution to the problem of the new postal receipt, Sir Rowland Hill had sought the help of three Royal Academicians, though he himself had found the right answer; and there are countless examples of advice being taken from outside sources for most issues of stamps.

But inevitably this advice tended to be Fine Art based. Admittedly, it would not have been easy for the Post Office to find many authorities on what we, today, refer to as industrial design; and although industrial designers began to exert an influence between the two wars, it was the years from 1939 to 1946 which really prepared the way for the establishment of design in the industrial scene.

It was Dr Hugh Dalton who, as President of the Board of Trade, in 1944 appointed (in the words of Hansard) 'A Council of Industrial Design to promote by all practicable means the improvement of design in the products of British industry.'

It speaks well of the Post Office that on the first occasion of a new issue of stamps after the end of the war – the Victory issue – it should ask the COID to suggest names of artists to be invited to submit designs. It is of some interest however that only after the intervention of the then President of the Board of Trade, Sir Stafford Cripps, was the COID allowed 'to advise on the final selection for submission to the King.' Making this request to the PMG, Sir Stafford apologized for not raising this question in Cabinet that same day and ended with this rather charming plea on behalf of his new baby: 'I hope you will be able to agree to this. The Council is a young body with its way to make in a difficult world and I am very anxious that they should have all possible encouragement.'

In many respects the Post Office attitude was understandable, for the

4/1 The 3d and 2½d Victory stamps: lack of design co-ordination

PMG had his own independent Advisory Panel consisting of Garter King of Arms, the Director of the National Gallery, and the Royal Fine Art Commission for Scotland. The COID's function, therefore, was seen only as one of recommending names of designers to the Post Office, but having no authority or influence on what designs were ultimately submitted to the King. Indeed it was some years before the Post Office was prepared to forego its assumption that the PMG with his Advisory Panel could alter, amend or add to the COID's selection at will and to accept that the Council was the overriding consultative body.

Without having any formal structure for selection, the COID asked Sir Francis Meynell, Typographical Adviser to the PMG, Sir Kenneth Clark and Sir Sydney Cockerell to form an *ad hoc* committee for this Victory issue. Unfortunately the hopeful start of this new association suffered a setback when the Post Office, rather autocratically, submitted – and ultimately issued – a design, the 2½d, which the COID had not seen. It also made matters worse by issuing to the Press a notice associating the names of the three COID judges with a stamp they had not chosen. In his reply to the inevitable complaint, the PMG Lord Listowel, admitted to the COID that he had been advised by three separate bodies: the COID, the Royal Fine Art Commission for Scotland and his own Advisory Panel.

But what really upset the COID was the fact that a change in the original brief for this issue had not been conveyed to its three judges. The PMG had said at first that he would be issuing stamps of two values but with the same design; eventually, however, he submitted three different essays to the Palace from which the King was to choose two. The COID team had been quite specific in its recommendation, remarking that the only drawing which had any merit of being a design, in the proper sense, was Reynolds Stone's. They were reluctant to name an alternative, but on being pressed, recommended one of Edmund Dulac's designs. 'Apart from Stone's, all designs tottered, but Dulac's number 5 might be said to walk.' In the end, the Post Office submitted designs by Stone, Dulac and Palmer, of Harrisons; two were chosen, one for each of the two values.

When the designs were published in the Press, it was seen that the one which had received the majority vote from all the advisers was given the 3d, or overseas, rate.

In a letter to *The Times* of 21 June 1946 John Carter, the well-known bibliophile asked:

'Can there be any doubt that the 3d Peace stamp is greatly superior in design to the 2½d? Surely not. Yet it will hardly be seen in this country,

the Empire or the United States and ten times as many of the others have
been printed. The difference in quality between the two stamps is so
striking that those interested in such things would welcome an expla-
nation of the principles which governed the choice: whether from the
Post Office or from the Council of Industrial Design, which advised on
the selection. For it is difficult to believe that the same judges could have
recommended both designs: Mr Stone's lapidary, calligraphic and
(within the imposed conditions) simple; Mr Palmer's, a confusion of
tints and symbols. The advantage of having two different designs is not
apparent: and if they represent a compromise between the differing
tastes of the Post Office and the Council, it is sad that the better stamp
should have been relegated to secondary uses.'

A disappointing beginning to what had promised to be a productive
association. In the following year, 1947, a similar situation was allowed to
develop over the Silver Wedding issue, the Post Office again publicly
associating the COID's advice with a stamp submitted by Harrisons, the
printers, which the COID had not approved. The only hopeful sign in that
year was the withdrawal of the Scottish Fine Art Commission from the
advisory position in favour of the COID.

The Council's association with the Post Office, which lasted for well-
nigh a quarter of a century, was punctuated by minor disagreements of this
nature; rarely serious enough to cause a breach at the time, but always
calling in question points of principle which, in the end, brought about a
complete severance.

In 1947, the COID formally constituted its Stamps Advisory Committee
with Sir Francis Meynell in the Chair and with the addition of the Keeper
of the Victoria & Albert Museum, Sir Leigh Ashton. That same year Sir
Francis made a formal request to Lord Listowel, the PMG, for a meeting
between the COID Committee and PMG's Advisory Panel in session,
giving as his reason the far from satisfactory situation arising from the fact
that his Committee was subject to an overriding authority, of whose
processes it was ignorant.

As nothing came of these overtures, a further request was made the
following year by the COID Director, Sir Gordon Russell, only to be met
with a blank refusal. In his reply, Mr Yates, Director of Postal Services, is
minuted as saying that 'it was the privilege of the PMG himself to advise
His Majesty, and the PMG was responsible publicly to Parliament for
stamp matters. His Advisory Panel might be found to express an overwhelming preference for one design and this would be reported to His

Majesty. If they wished for any reason to exclude a design of the COID's choice, it would be told of it.' He did, however, go on to say that an aggregate of the choice of both bodies had often been offered to His Majesty as alternative designs not selected by the Council. From now on no such designs would reach His Majesty, although the Council would be asked always to choose a couple of designs in excess of the number to be used, to leave His Majesty some choice.

This indeed was progress, even though it did not remove the anomaly of the COID's advice being monitored by another consultative body with whom they had no contact. It took a further seven years for this sought-after meeting to be achieved and even when it happened it was a failure. The meeting proved to be quite unmanageable, since all the members were assumed to have equal authority on design, which was far from the case. Besides, the COID Committee found it well-nigh impossible to put forward a coherent judgement at so large a meeting, especially when they had not previously seen the designs under consideration.

In May 1952 the COID Committee was reconstituted to deal with the first stamps of the new reign; the Coronation issue (see p. 78) and the new definitive range. Lady Sempill, Sir Kenneth Clark, Sir Leigh Ashton and Sir John Wilson, Keeper of the Queen's Philatelic collection, consented to serve, with Sir Francis Meynell remaining Chairman. The previous year, Sir Kenneth Clark had been invited to join the PMG's Advisory Panel, an appointment which proved of great value to the COID Committee.

Four years later, however, the PMG's Advisory Panel lapsed not to be reconstituted, under a different format, until 1967. The role of the COID Committee became, therefore, of paramount importance, particularly in the eyes of professional designers who were quick to react.

By March 1957, encouraged no doubt by a letter from Abram Games in the December 1956 issue of *Design* magazine, the Society of Industrial Artists was becoming restive at what it considered to be the rather less than professional behaviour of the Advisory Committee. The SIA was mainly concerned at the insufficient representation by practising designers, at the unknown composition of the Committee, and the fact that too many designs were commissioned and fees were too low. They were also uneasy at the degree of design direction being given to designers (a misconception as it happened). A meeting was held therefore between a group of SIA members who had been involved in stamp design and Sir Gordon Russell and it was agreed that Lynton Lamb and Abram Games be appointed to the Panel to represent the SIA. This paved the way for other designers to be co-opted over the years, so strengthening the professional voice.

By November 1957, however, the relationship between the COID and the Post Office was a matter of such concern to Sir Gordon Russell and Sir Francis Meynell, that a meeting was held with S. D. Sargent, Deputy General at the GPO, to discuss informally the selection procedures which everyone felt to be unsatisfactory. As a result of that meeting Mr Sargent promised to discuss with the Assistant PMG, Mr Kenneth Thompson, the following points; more careful briefing of designers, if possible at a meeting; a new integrated committee; a smaller number of contestants and better paid; fewer submissions by printers of work commissioned from freelance designers, and a preview of the designs by the Committee.

In a memorandum from the PMG, dated 29 April 1958, the following points were made and modifications to procedure outlined.

'Sir Francis Meynell and Sir Gordon Russell have felt some concern about the working of the arrangements for obtaining stamp designs from artists and for advising the PMG on the designs submitted. They were particularly concerned with the necessity of ensuring that: (a) artistic advice should be properly formulated and given satisfactory hearing – an objective which may not easily be attained at a large meeting attended by a number of people with no special qualifications in the artistic field, and (b) the artists work under conditions likely to produce the highest possible standard.'

Among the procedural changes it was proposed that at meetings of the Minister and his officials with the COID Committee (now called the Advisory Panel) no one else would normally be present, except Garter King of Arms. Designs would be sent to members of the Advisory Panel before meetings. A meeting with the sponsors and the printers would be held with the Post Office to ensure that due account was taken of printing factors and communicated to the Advisory Panel.

As regards the conditions under which artists work, it was agreed that the total number of designs submitted and the number of artists commissioned should be reduced and that one new name should appear on the short list for every issue, so as not to restrict stamp design to a small circle. The printers would be invited to submit, but restricted to the same number of artists. Amateurs would not be invited to submit designs. Artists would be given every opportunity to question and clarify points arising out of the briefing. The rough drawing stage would be eliminated.

It was also agreed that the PMG would always be free not to avail himself of the Advisory Panel's advice; or, having received the advice, make a different recommendation to His Majesty. Where the Advisory

Panel were not involved in an issue, care would be taken that their names would not appear in any publicity connected with that issue. So far so good. Not ideal, but a great improvement on the old arrangements.

Amongst Sir Francis Meynell's papers, now in the University Library in Cambridge, I found a copy of his charming letter, dated 8 October 1958, to Sir Gordon Russell, after they completed this 'New Deal' as he called it.

'Now that we have come to this very happy conclusion with Sargent about future procedure for stamp competitions, the perfect moment has arrived for me to retire from the Advisory Panel. As you know I have had this in mind for some time, partly to ease myself, because I am half-retired and more than half-tired, but also because it is time for a youthful succession. The new procedure will have more meaning and encouragement for the designers if you reduce the average age of the Committee, which my departure will ensure!

I lately retired from cricket, and had the luck to finish with a decent score, a good catch and (even more important from the point of view of sympathy and admiration) a split finger! The "New Deal" is almost as good a finale: though you have never called on me to suffer for the side . . . I thank you, and will you for me thank the Council, and wish all success to my successor?'

The 'New Deal' formed the basis of the relationship between the two bodies for the next few years, until, in 1961, a further memorandum was drawn up on similar lines, but tightening up the coordination between the Post Office, the sponsors, the printers and the Advisory Panel, and endeavouring to allow more time for the designer to do his work and the Panel to make its recommendations. In the same year two new members were co-opted to the Panel, Milner Gray and myself. James Fitton had also joined in 1956.

For some time the COID had been seeking ways to make good the lack of professional design control within the Post Office and in the summer of 1962 it suggested two modifications to the current procedures. The first, that they should revert to an earlier plan whereby designers would submit preliminary designs; and the second, that having selected those designs which were worthy of development, a designer member of the Panel should act as design director and, with the stamp designer, carry the design through to the final stage, taking into account all the requirements of the Post Office and the Panel.

But the Post Office would not agree, arguing that such a procedure would reduce the 'artists' to the level of draughtsmen. 'We don't pay high fees for this,' was the answer. An odd reaction, but in a way understandable, for there was still this belief that the 'artist', as he was called, acted on some sort of divine inspiration and the idea that a design solution could best be worked out through the closest co-operation of client, designer and printer was quite unknown.

A further memorandum was drawn up the same year and remained in effect until the Panel was disbanded five years later, but it did not provide the complete solution to the Panel's difficulties, among which were listed at the time the unpredictable performance on the part of some good designers; the insufficient time allowed for the development of designs (especially in 1964–65 when there were nine issues); the insufficient liaison between the sponsors, the GPO and the Panel, resulting in changes of mind on the part of the sponsors on seeing the designs; the GPO's opposition to the 'art direction' of artists lest their style be cramped; the spontaneous intervention on the part of the Postmaster General and the absence of design-minded officials in the Post Services Department. 'Our opposite numbers in the GPO' complained the COID Secretariat 'are non-specialized and have much other work.'

But if the COID was finding life with the Post Office at times rather frustrating, the Stamp Advisory Panel found a new interest to occupy its attention. In May 1961 Sir Kenneth Clark had suggested that the COID should organize an exhibition of international stamps, selected solely on their design qualities. The exhibition would be organized on the basis of subject categories, rather than by country, so that it would be possible to compare different treatments of the same subject by different postal administrations.

Edgar Lewy, a well-known philatelist who had been making critical noises in the Press at the low standard of design of Commonwealth stamps, was commissioned to carry out a preliminary selection from stamps issued over the past forty years. He submitted nearly 1,200 stamps and I was given the job of choosing the 300 to 400 which I considered to be of high design standard. I was also expected to be able to justify my selection to the Panel, which had already agreed that, if the exhibition was to do any good at all, we should be able to explain very simply why certain stamps had been chosen.

The exhibition comprised such thematic subjects as Royal portraits, other portraits, architectural subjects, flora and fauna, heraldic devices and emblems, and sport; it also included brief notes on the printing processes.

This was the first time that an exhibition of postage stamps had ever been assembled against these criteria; as the introduction proclaimed, postage stamps were selected for their qualities of design and not for their philatelic value. The selectors thought that a well-designed stamp should show:

> '(a) good composition, (b) good design and drawing detail, (c) clear statements of purpose, value and nationality, (d) proper exploitation of the process of reproduction.'

It is not easy to assess the true value of such an exercise; but at least those responsible for United Kingdom stamp production, the Post Office and the Stamp Advisory Panel, had for the first time the opportunity to make a comparison between the standards of our own administration and those of others. Much as I was intrigued by the overall job of selection, I was amazed how difficult it was to find a good showing of United Kingdom stamps. What I found depressing was the sad comparison which they made with some of our European friends. As Edgar Lewy put it, writing in the July 1962 issue of *Gibbons Stamp Monthly*, 'In the very nature of things, the exhibition (carefully arranged and mounted though it was) could not but indicate how the problem is solved in other places. The Establishment of philately was present at the opening; did they draw any conclusion from what they saw, or indeed (and even more to the point) did they read the lessons which were presented to them on the walls?'

Who can tell? But of this one can be sure. In the years that followed, the design of postage stamps began to rate much higher in the thinking of officials at the Post Office as well as at the Council of Industrial Design.

Not only did the annual number of issues increase, but the newly-found ability of Harrisons to print stamps in multi-colour for the first time in 1963 brought a new freedom to stamp design. At the same time, there was beginning to appear a certain relaxation from some of the official restrictions which had tended to inhibit design, such as the inclusion of the portrait of a commoner alongside that of the Queen, as in the Shakespeare issue of 1964 and the Churchill stamps a year later (see p. 68).

Two years later saw the arrival at the Post Office of Anthony Wedgwood Benn as Postmaster General, and from that moment on things were never to be the same again.

5 Liberalizing stamp policy

Much of what Tony Benn achieved during those two years was to have a profound effect on postage stamp design thinking, although the methods he adopted were at times called into question.

For example, it is difficult to understand why the brief given to David Gentleman for the preparation of his design album covered much the same ground as the terms of reference laid down for Andrew Restall's Fellowship in Minuscule Design at the Royal College of Art.

In a press release prepared for the Stamp Seminar on 23 June 1966, at which David Gentleman's album was first made public, this statement appeared: 'David Gentleman, in response to this general invitation (Hansard, 15 December 1964) wrote a long memorandum outlining ways in which he thought British stamp policy might develop. He was commissioned to illustrate his thesis by preparing an album of experimental designs. The idea of this exercise was to produce something experimental that committed neither the Post Office nor anyone else to accept what was submitted.' And this is the PMG's brief, of April 1965, to Andrew Restall:

'(a) To review the whole field of minuscule design with reference to postage and national savings stamps and related matters.

(b) To study the opportunities offered by modern symbolism and imagery for more effective recognition, communication, prestige and security in miniature design in this field.

(c) To explore new techniques and materials.

(d) To prepare a report, including exemplary designs, on which a national policy might be based.'

Admittedly the terms of reference for the Research Fellowship allow for a deeper study, but it is difficult to appreciate what was expected from these two exercises that did not create duplication.

After Andrew Restall had been at work at the College for some months, the situation disturbed both him and the COID to the extent that the Council wrote to the PMG, drawing his attention to this overlap, and reminding him that much of the work at the College could be vitiated by the too early publication of David Gentleman's recommendations.

In the event, the main interest in the Gentleman album was centred on one aspect of his study which Andrew Restall did not pursue, even though his terms of reference allowed him to do so: the search for a graphic element with which to identify United Kingdom stamps, other than by the Sovereign's head.

David Gentleman held very strongly to the view, and indeed it was one of the main points in his letter to the PMG, that better design standards

could be achieved if an alternative element to the sovereign's head could
be found, which could be integrated more happily with other pictorial or
graphic elements. The obligatory use of the Dorothy Wilding 'proper'
photographic portrait did create an extremely difficult design problem,
especially as the Post Office insisted that the head should be no smaller
than that on the definitive stamps. This rule began to be relaxed around
1963, but it did not wholly cure the problem. Therefore Gentleman
experimented with royal cyphers and coats of arms, all in silhouette. And
some of his experimental designs looked very nice, but he admits now that
the significant thing about a coat of arms is all the heraldic detail within the
shield which certainly would not have appeared in the silhouette, and
although he was content then to use it as a decorative element, he is not
sure now that it had the necessary significance.

Nor am I so sure that the Post Office could have sustained such a break
with precedence as a member of the UPU, and I certainly did not share
Tony Benn's optimism on this point.

But in any event, there was a solution just round the corner which in the
end Gentleman adopted: to draw a silhouette head based on the Mary
Gillick coinage head. This he did and it was first used on the Landscapes
issue of May 1966.

5/1 Dorothy Wilding's portrait
on a definitive and on a
commemorative of 1961

5/2 The Wilding portrait down
in size: still not the perfect
solution

5/3 Some of David Gentleman's silhouette drawings and their application to experimental stamp design

In many respects it was a great pity that this compromise did not present itself earlier in the study, for the rumour that experiments were in hand to find a replacement for the sovereign's effigy not unexpectedly was interpreted in quite the wrong way; it acquired a political significance which was attributed more to the PMG's left-wing tendencies than to his design interests. Matters were only made worse when the Stamp Advisory Panel was told that the Robert Burns issue was to be designed with and without the Queen's head. When it was also told that the designs would be essayed both ways, the Chairman, Sir Kenneth Clark, retorted that as far as he was concerned, until he was told officially to the contrary, the inclusion of the Sovereign's head was obligatory. All very tiresome and as it turned out quite unnecessary. Needless to say Robert Burns and the Battle of Britain sets were both issued in the normal way.

In October 1965 Sir Kenneth Clark resigned the Chairmanship of the Panel on the grounds that he had served long enough. It was suggested at the time that he was reluctant to be placed in the position of having to recommend to the Queen stamps which did not bear her effigy. I recently asked Lord Clark whether there was any substance in this suggestion. 'I was perfectly sincere' he wrote, 'when I said that I resigned because I had held it long enough, but the words can be interpreted in various ways.

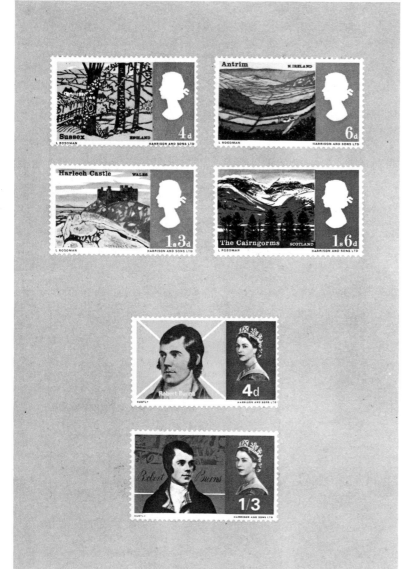

5/4 Gentleman's silhouette head on the Landscapes issue of 1966

5/5 The final Robert Burns issue; experimental designs covered the whole surface of the stamp and omitted the Queen's head

5/6 The Battle of Britain
stamps as finally issued: with the
Queen's head

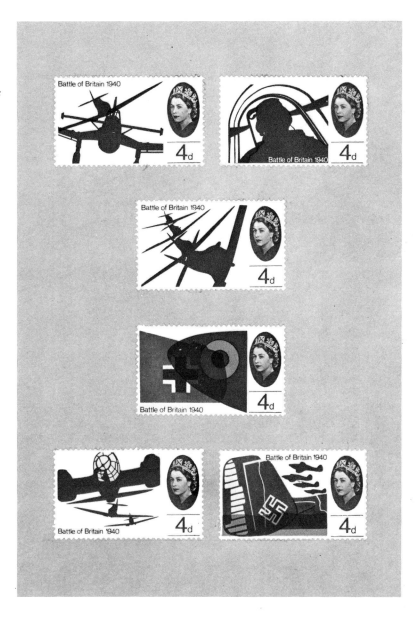

5/7 Gentleman's Railway designs   LIVERPOOL AND MANCHESTER RAILWAY 1830   LIVERPOOL AND MANCHESTER RAIL

There had been a change of outlook in the production of stamps with
which I was not in sympathy. I cannot say if I was right or wrong but it was
evident to me that there should be a Chairman with more liberal views. I
was afraid that the admission of pictorial stamps would lead to complete
banality, and I have been proved right. What about the last two issues?
Moreover, I believe that pictorial stamps are wrong in principle. A stamp
should have the character of a crest or badge with some symbolic meaning.
This was strongly the opinion of that great stamp collector, George V, who
often discussed the matter with me. I would like to have heard his comments on both the new 10p.'

Then in a postscript he added: 'I should have enjoyed even more King
George's comments on the new 9p stamp. Is it not a complete surrender
that the country of Shakespeare should have chosen for its subject Jemima
Puddleduck and Peter Rabbit?'

The issues to which Lord Clark refers were Horseracing (see p. 89) and
the Year of the Child (see p. 16), both in 1979.

The Gentleman album did contain some lovely stamps, but inevitably
they were based on thematic subjects not on anniversaries and I know only
of one experimental design which ultimately found its way into the issuing
programme, with some modifications, that delightful set of five railway
carriages which together make up a train. It was used on the Liverpool–
Manchester Railway issue in March 1980.

Whether the designs in the album influenced Post Office policy to the
extent of suggesting other subjects for later issues, is difficult to say, for some
of the themes David Gentleman included did find their way into publication; trees, the Stubbs 'Mares and foals' and architecture. Certainly the
new format that he used, that of $1:\sqrt{2}$, was later adopted for all commemorative stamps and it was always referred to as the 'Gentleman size'.

Those designers who may have seen reproductions of the album, must
have been influenced by the new disposition of the Queen's effigy in its
silhouette form; it undoubtedly affected David Gentleman's subsequent
approach to his own designs.

The result of Andrew Restall's Fellowship, in the end, took a different
turn. He published three reports. The first on 4 April 1967 on *The relative
merits of different printing processes*, the second on 28 April on *Some relevant
factors in considering the size of postage stamps*, and finally *Aims and recommendations* in September 1967.

In his introduction to this final report, Andrew Restall states very clearly
where his real interests lay. 'The purpose of this report is to formulate,
within the terms of the brief, a new policy for British stamp design from the

viewpoint of the designer. The report is therefore concerned with all the events leading to the issue of a new stamp which affect the designer and his brief, and thus the appearance of the stamp.

As with other fields of design, a successful policy depends as much on the enlightened support of the client (in this case the General Post Office) as on the calibre of the individual designers concerned. It is thus particularly important that decisions of a policy nature are taken with as full as possible an understanding of design matters, and it is hoped that the report will go some way towards achieving this.'

Not surprisingly, therefore, his study was concerned primarily with determining new methods of design management to create a more professional relationship between the Post Office and the designer. This is not to say that he did not embark on some fundamental research into the operational requirements of a stamp and the design qualities that most affect the result.

He was involved, too, along with a number of other designers in the search for a new definitive stamp and a new portrait of the Queen, yet it is surprising that there seemed to have been no attempt to co-ordinate their work. Some of his results were most interesting, but later he admitted to feeling uneasy about the risk of seeming to lay down guide lines for stamp design. 'I felt it would be dangerous for me to provide the Post Office with a do-it-yourself guide to stamp designing, because that is not the way it is done.'

He also got himself involved in the search for a new definitive and a new identifying design element, but the conclusions he drew were both logical and sensible. Taking the extreme literary identification of the country of origin as 'United Kingdom of Great Britain, Northern Ireland and the Channel Islands' he quickly dismissed it as an impracticable design solution. He made no reference to 'UK Postage' which appeared on the Robert Burns essays. Similarly he found insurmountable difficulties for the Scots in the use of the Royal Coat of Arms, the Royal cypher and the Crown itself, for there is a quite distinct Scottish version of all these heraldic elements which the Scots would insist on using. 'The conclusion is inevitably reached,' he wrote, 'that the head is the only way of satisfying the needs of all'. 'But' he continued, 'what has not yet been attempted is a version of the Queen's head designed especially for incorporation with pictorials. The ideal situation would be one in which a basic "master" head existed and the choice of treatment of this master would be the individual designer's. We now have a three-dimensional master for the definitive series. The possibility of using a similar head as a master for

5/8 Some of the designs
produced by Andrew Restall's
students

the pictorials is worth serious consideration. By this means we would retain
the uniformity required, and gain the versatility the designer needs.' To
this end he included a number of possible treatments in the Appendix to
his report.

It is however the prime recommendation in the report that makes the
most interesting reading, that of an improved design management structure within the Post Office. Andrew Restall had had experience of working
with the Post Office, having designed stamps in four issues over the
previous three years. So he had some knowledge of the procedures and the
way they affected the final outcome. He started by listing seven stages in
the design process where decisions are taken and he isolated three which, in
his view, are key stages; preparing the brief, choosing the designs, and
making the final choice. At all these stages, he claimed, 'decisions are taken
by different bodies who, far from consulting each other to consider overall
policy, are indeed vigorous guardians of their own independence.' He
admitted that they all have considerable specialist experience, but in most

cases no professional design experience. This echoed the constant complaint of the COID Advisory Panel.

Restall sought to remedy this lack of co-ordination by the appointment of a stamp design director. He then re-cast those same seven stages with the added involvement of the design director. It is a well-thought out structure and one which would have attracted a deal of attention and maybe support, as well as making for a much better relationship between the Post Office and the designer. However, by the time Andrew Restall's report was in the Post Office hands the decision to appoint a design director had already been taken.

If ever a good idea had been allowed to go to waste, surely this Fellowship in Minuscule Design must be a classic. It had been set up with hardly any consultation between those responsible for implementing the results of the study, the Operations and Overseas Department at the Post Office and the COID. No formal link had been established between the Post Office and the Royal College of Art, at a workaday level, to ensure that the research was kept within reasonable operational limits. Indeed, not only was there no positive link, but Andrew Restall sensed an attitude of indifference, almost hostility, towards what he was trying to achieve. But

5/9 The search for a new definitive: proposals from David Gentleman using photographs by John Hedgecoe

he did have enthusiastic and active support from a group of students working with him at the College, some of whom produced very promising work. And, of course, by the time he was able to make his report, the Postmaster General who had instituted the Fellowship had been moved and his place taken by another.

On 23 June 1966 the PMG, Anthony Wedgwood Benn, held a Stamps Seminar to which he had invited members of the Stamp Advisory Panel, leading stamp designers, the design, art and philatelic representatives of the leading firms of printers of postage stamps, representatives of the dealers' associations and of the philatelic bodies. As the Press Release put it, 'the first purpose of the Seminar is to lift from the subject of stamp design some of the secrecy that had traditionally clothed it.'

Much was made of the new liberalized policy of stamp production which was the hall-mark of the new ministerial administration and this was supported by a display of David Gentleman's album, references to Andrew Restall's Fellowship at the Royal College of Art, some examples of 'Colourful British Stamps' and the Battle of Britain, essays of commemorative stamps issued between 1924 and the end of 1965, original designs by the top six artists, a selection of Children's Christmas stamp designs, designs by Jock Kinneir for small pictorials, and 'Specimen Crown Agents Stamps, showing Royal cyphers and symbols – no Queen's head.'

As a public relations exercise the Seminar was an undoubted success, although the contributions made by those who attended added little beyond saying what a good boy the Post Office was. It did, of course commit the Post Office to a much closer involvement with the philatelic trade and confirmed the view that the Post Office was now in the stamps promotion game up to the neck. At the time that seemed a good thing; whether more recent history has confirmed that view or not is a matter for conjecture. Perhaps what was not fully realized at the time was the very high standard of design the Post Office considered to be essential to the proper implementation of the new stamp issuing policy. When he first arrived, Wedgwood Benn had made it known that he intended to promote a new image of the Post Office through its stamps. And this he undoubtedly did, at the same time enabling stamps, by the very quality of their design, to make a useful profit for the Post Office. Later, alas, the pursuit of even greater profits threatened to erode those standards.

A few weeks later a new Postmaster General arrived, Edward Short, MP, and a new chapter in the long saga of British stamp design and production was about to open.

6 PMG extraordinary

I recently went to see Tony Benn, MP, who of all Postmasters General had, in his short time at the Post Office, done more than anyone else to stimulate interest in stamp design and production. I asked him to recall those decisions, successful or otherwise, which he remembers most lovingly.

TB: 'If I can begin at the beginning, I was in any case most interested in design and had been for some time. When I became PMG in 1964 I began by sending a series of minutes to the Director General of the Post Office, Sir Ronald Germain, and I remember an early one which asked him to prepare a Post Office Christmas card which we could sell. This would partly raise revenue, and would also experiment with a new official card of a different kind. And, if we were to hold a competition for the design of these cards, we could encourage British artists to take part and give the Post Office the opportunity to provide public patronage of the Arts.

'Later that month I mentioned at a Board meeting that I was considering the establishment of a research fellowship in minuscule design at some appropriate institution. If we were to expand our stamp programme, which I very much wanted to do, then we should also think of ways in which we could increase the number of designers competent to execute it.

'Then, in December 1964, in a written reply to Rafton Pounder who had asked me about the new criteria of determining Commemorative issues, and on what occasions in 1965 would they be issued, I gave my new criteria: "to celebrate events of national and international importance, to commemorate important anniversaries, to reflect the British contribution to world affairs including the arts and sciences and to extend public patronage to the arts by encouraging the development of minuscule art." To this I added: "In the general interest the number of special issues should be kept within reasonable bounds and I intend to limit this number to eight in the next twelve months, each consisting of two stamps", then, and this was the key paragraph: "In the preparation of lists for consideration it would be helpful if Rt. Hon. and Hon. members and members of the public would submit suggestions to me as quickly as possible, since the decisions for 1965 will have to be reached early in January. At the same time it would also be helpful to receive the views of those who are interested in stamp design policy generally."

'Now I regard that last sentence as the key. I had felt for a long time that there were lots of people with ideas, not only in the Arts, who were being held back by bureaucrats in various organizations including the Post Office, and that if you could give them the signal they would welcome the opportunity to put up those ideas. This could produce a great flowering – the 100 flowers or whatever.

'David Gentleman wrote to me, along with a number of others, to say that he had many ideas about postage stamp design. I appointed him to prepare an album of designs for subjects which the Post Office could issue as special stamps. At the same time I arranged for Andrew Restall to take up a Research Fellowship at the Royal College of Art.

'The next problem was to get the Post Office to accept that the Post-master General had any right to be interested in stamp design; because they had a system under which stamps were essayed, sent to me and I trans-mitted them with a respectful note to Sir Michael Adeane at the Palace, who would then show them to the Queen and the response would come back by the same route.

'I did have a link with the Council of Industrial Design through their Stamps Advisory Panel, but they did not think that the PMG should do more than indicate some ideas for Commemorative stamps – but not too many! And as for design itself, he should stay absolutely clear and let design be dealt with on a professional basis.

6/1 The Churchill issue: contrast and controversy

'I wanted more stamps and I wanted a wider range of designs. That was how it began. Next I had to clear my way with the Palace for these new designs. The first occasion arose after the death of Sir Winston Churchill. The Post Office objected that there had never been another head on the stamp as well as the Sovereign's. The Palace agreed to the design. But of course the two heads fitted very uneasily with one another because they were both literal heads. David Gentleman had designed the Churchillian head to dominate, with the Queen's head almost fitted in over his shoulder.

'The next stamp that caused controversy was the Battle of Britain commemorative. First because there were a lot of stamps in the issue, but more because one bore the swastika. There was a flaming row and I had lots of letters and press criticism about it. Actually the swastika is shown on a German bomber submerged in the sea after being shot down by four Spitfires seen above it. I think really it was the novelty of the issue that caused the upset.

'Another stamp which led to an argument was the one commemorating Robbie Burns (see p. 61). Because of his private life there were some who thought he should never have appeared on the same stamp with the Queen, particularly when in one of them he appears to be looking at her.'

SR: 'I'd forgotten, we nearly lost Nellie O'Brien in the issue of Reynolds paintings in 1973 (see p. 88) for much the same reason. The Director of Marketing thought it improper for a lady of her character to share a stamp with the Queen. Fortunately she was saved by the Chairman of the Trustees of the Tate Gallery, who was a member of the Stamp Advisory

Committee, on the grounds that we were commemorating the skills of the painter and not the morals of the sitter.'

TB: 'People are very sensitive about this sort of thing. I believe there was a row in 1840, when the first adhesive stamp was brought in, at the thought of people licking the back of the Queen's head!

'The Dorothy Wilding photographic head of the Queen did create problems until David Gentleman drew a miniature silhouette version, so it could be used as a design element.'

SR: 'This new head grew out of David's album, because it predates Arnold Machin's new definitives.'

TB: 'Yes, he had put in a plan for new definitives based on photographs which were not adopted. Then Arnold Machin produced this lovely relief picture and I got that agreed as well, though it was a slightly sensitive issue because one seemed to suggest that the Dorothy Wilding picture of the young queen was no longer appropriate. But the new definitive head was even better. In the end the miniature white silhouette used on commemoratives, and known irreverently as the "Camay soap" head, was replaced by the much more attractive ones in black and gold. Later, of course, the Gentleman designs became predominant.

6/2 The 'Camay soap' head on the Birds issue of 1966

'I'll tell you an amusing thing about the Concorde stamps. The highest value was prepared at the first class mail rate, but the first flight of Concorde and the stamps were delayed for a year. By the time it eventually took off, the Post Office had put up the postage rate making the old First Class rate Second Class. I was told "You cannot have a supersonic aircraft stamp carrying only Second Class mail." They had forgotten however that the stamp carried a phosphor bar which automatically sorted it into the first class stream. When, therefore, you bought a Concorde stamp you got a first class postal service for the price of a second class stamp. About a week before I left the Post Office, in June 1966, we had the Stamp Seminar, which you attended. By then, of course, the new designs had been tremendously successful and admired all over the world. They had provided scope for a new art form, from this country's point of view, and the development of artistic possibilities that were simply prevented from being expressed in the old days. I had also put in some new proposals, one of them being for a Charity Stamp whereby the Post Office would provide a stamp with a face value lower than what you paid for it and would give the difference to charity and supplement the Christmas seals. That, in a nutshell, was the story while I was at the Post Office in 1964–1966.

'In 1974 I found myself Minister of Posts and Telecommunications again and I wanted a stamp for the American Bicentennial, or Bicentenary as we would call it. The Managing Director Posts replied to this suggestion: "Although the Bicentenary of the Declaration of Independence by the thirteen American Colonies has the support of the Foreign and Commonwealth Office, it is our view that this subject is not suitable for inclusion in the special stamp programme. However it might be approached in design terms, there would be a danger that ordinary people would criticise the issue as celebrating a defeat. Moreover there could well be feeling in those former British Colonies which achieved independence later and without bloodshed that, whilst for instance we did not mark the centenary of the British North America Act of 1867, we should seem to honour those who rebelled." Now that shows how bureaucracy, two hundred years after American Independence, still treated America as a rebel colony. I think in the end they did produce stamps for the Bicentenary didn't they?'

6/3 The stamp that missed its value (or the plane that missed the boat)

SR: 'Yes, one. It was quite nice. We had photographed the bust of Benjamin Franklin, which is in the Royal Society of Arts, because we had awful trouble in finding a suitable design. There was a very close association, through Franklin and the RSA, with the States and he was, after all, their first Postmaster General.'

TB: 'You see, I think it is very significant that they wouldn't honour Washington, the first President. I remember we had a very amusing discussion in the Government about how we might celebrate the American Bicentenary and in the end I think we gave them a facsimile of Magna Carta. I suggested that we should repeal the legislation under which they were declared rebels and pass a formal Bill giving them their independence. There was a lot of chuntering among Ministers and somebody said, "It might not get through the House." Let me give another example, also from 1974. I wanted a Trade Union stamp and was told: "You can't have a Trade Union stamp because it would come out in 1976, the anniversary of the General Strike." So they put the Trade Union movement into the issue on Great British Institutions – they didn't call it Trade Unionism.'

6/4 The American Bicentenary issue

SR: 'Social Reformers in fact.' (See also p. 118–19.)

TB: 'They picked Thomas Hepburn, but they made no reference to the fact that he was the Secretary of the Northumberland Miners. They were prepared to do religions, flowers, trains, artists but they would not admit to the existence of Trade Unionism as such.'

SR: 'The Post Office was tied to a policy of commemorating people or events and there had to be a good apparent reason for an issue. As far as I can recall there was no significant birthday event that could justify the publication of a Trade Union issue at that date.'

6/5 Arnold Machin's bas-relief portrait

TB: 'Well, 1926 was the General Strike and I suppose I should have asked for the 50th Anniversary of the General Strike.'

SR: 'That would have been in 1976. You had asked for the stamp to be published in 1975 when the programme was full up and it was issued the year after.'

TB: 'I think the Committee was conservative in design terms and was prepared to celebrate all sorts of things, like sailing. Did Heath ask for that one?'

SR: 'No, the reason for the issue was the 200th Anniversary of the Royal Thames Yacht Club, Britain's oldest Sailing Club. In the event, the issue turns out to be a set of stamps about sailing.' (See also p. 114–15.)

TB: 'I must be honest with you, that didn't actually convince me.'

SR: 'I turned up some Battle of Britain essays the other day without the Queen's head on. Were they ever submitted to the Palace?'

TB: 'Yes, because six portrait heads on six stamps all joined together in a way highlighted the design problem. This did not apply with the silhouette head on the Battle of Hastings stamps where the head was shown as a design feature.'

SR: 'Did anyone pursue the implication of replacing the Queen's head with something else? David Gentleman tried using the Coat of Arms. Would that in fact have satisfied the Universal Postal Union, because there was no precedent for it as there was with the Sovereign's head?'

TB: 'There were two arguments used against it. One, that as we had always had the Sovereign's head as an identifying feature we were exempted from UPU regulations. The other argument, equally valid, was that as we had invented the adhesive postage stamp, whatever we did was all right. I took the latter view, but one might argue that it was very undesirable to change the head for the cypher. Because of our special position in the UPU nobody would dream of trying to contradict our standing in the matter. But the whole thing became very political, though actually in my mind it was entirely a design matter.

'I don't know if you ever saw the stamps that were based simply on a signature?'

SR: 'Yes, indeed, one of the Robbie Burns essays without the Queen's head but "UK Postage" instead. Very American-looking.'

TB: 'I've never seen a signature on a stamp, but do they use them in America? The thing about a Burns signature is that the writer's main characteristic is his signature and therefore the picture of a writer is less important than his writing.

'I found the Post Office a fascinating organization. The management

6/6 The Thomas Hepburn
stamp, one among the Social
Reformers

6/7 Sailing, for the
200th Anniversary of the Royal
Thames Yacht Club

tradition was drawn from the Armed Forces – as it were, from the Royal Corps of Signals, absolutely disciplined and authoritarian. The Union of Postal Workers is the one Union committed to Guild Socialism, namely that they should run it themselves. Those two contradictory influences, like soldiers at the Trooping of the Colour, marched and counter-marched through each other's ranks, turning and doing it again without any ill-will or hostility. They were all utterly devoted to the Post Office, as I am. But there was never really any meeting of minds between the management and the Unions. Everything was organized for the benefit of the Post Office and yet it had this fantastic reputation for reliable service. I love the Post Office. There is no organization like it in Britain.'

7 The new policies take shape

But what of the stamps which resulted from the somewhat uneasy association between the Post Office and the COID and to what extend did their differences affect the standard of design? Certainly the issues which appeared between 1946 and 1952 were not up to the same standard of, say, the Silver Jubilee set of 1935, the Coronation issue of 1937 or the Stamp Centenary stamp of 1940. It is of some interest that in the first two issues with which the COID was involved, the stamps which spoiled the sets, as sets, were the very designs which the COID had not seen nor approved: the $2\frac{1}{2}$d Victory and the $2\frac{1}{2}$d Silver Wedding (see p. 51). The remaining issues of that reign are not among the most distinguished stamps the Post Office has produced.

The fault, however, seems to lie in the method of selection. Both the COID selectors and the Postmaster General's Advisory Panel, more often than not, were put into the position of having to make a choice from a wide range of submissions, so although some issues may contain one or two well-designed individual stamps, they rarely hang together as a set. It seems as though it was a positive act of policy not to aim for consistency; even the high value issue of 1951 only makes a half-hearted concession to the unified set concept.

On the other hand, during the twenty-year life of the COID Panel, the Post Office issued some notable stamps over which the Panel had exerted a not inconsiderable influence. Certainly the older the Panel got the more mature was its judgement and it is possible to discern the improvements which resulted from the joint agreements on procedure in 1958 and 1961. Without doubt, the new reign marked the beginning of a new standard in stamp design which was to reach its peak in the 1970s.

Those early years of the reign are, from a design point of view, perhaps some of the most interesting. Coming so soon after the outstandingly successful Festival of Britain the year before, the Accession provided the opportunity for much of the design innovation and excitement to be channelled into this new Elizabethan age. Add to that the naturally emotional reaction to having a Queen as sovereign, and a young and glamorous one at that, and one felt a new sense of adventure nowhere less positive than in the world of design.

The 1951 Festival had given to a whole new generation of designers, many of them trained as architects, the chance to shed on one giant scheme all the frustrations to their professional careers, which the war had imposed, as well as the limitations of a peace which never seemed to materialize. The result was a potion so heady as to intoxicate the whole design profession. Against this background, therefore, the design of British stamps

7/1 The 1951 high value issue

takes on a rather different look from those which were issued during the reigns of the Queen's father and grandfather; and it is possible to trace the gradual development away from the traditional heraldic approach towards a more contemporary graphic design solution.

Work on the new definitive issue commenced a few days after the Accession, with the Queen sitting for a new series of photographs by Dorothy Wilding. The Post Office had already decided not to break with the historic tradition of making the portrait of the Sovereign the prime element of the stamp. Originally the Dorothy Wilding photographs had been taken as reference material from which Edmund Dulac was commissioned to make a drawing. In the end, however, one of a second series of photographs by Dorothy Wilding was accepted as final. The only departure from tradition was that this photograph was 'proper' (i.e. three-quarter profile) rather than 'formal' (full profile), a pose only used once before for the first stamps of George V in 1911. In the meantime the COID had recommended a number of designers who would submit designs for the issue using the new photograph. Initially three designs were envisaged and out of the 67 submitted nine were shortlisted by the Postmaster General's Advisory Panel. The Postmaster General's recommendation to the Queen

7/2 George V in 1911: proper portrait

7/3 The five different designs used in 1952 around the Wilding portrait

was for those designed by Enid Marx RDI, M. C. Farrar Bell, Mary Adshead and Edmund Dulac. The Queen approved the selection but with the addition of a design by one of Harrison's designers, G. Knipe.

In many respects the issue is unsatisfactory, for although all five designs conform in the main to a common pattern, that of the centrally-placed portrait surrounded by oval shapes, decoration and lettering, the differences in detailed treatment all tend to irritate rather than satisfy. Because of the variations in treatment, the portraits are marginally different in size; the typography is inconsistent and, with the exception of the Enid Marx design, the handling of the national flower emblems a bit obvious and commonplace.

It is tempting to make a comparison between this issue and the outstanding definitive set of 1937/50 by Eric Gill and Edmund Dulac (see also p. 27). Admittedly the 1953 definitives are very feminine, which is quite right and proper for a Queen's set of stamps; but maybe it is the 'proper' portrait of the Queen compared with the 'formal' portrait of her father that has robbed this issue of an inherent dignity. Unfortunately we had to wait another fourteen years, until 1967, for Arnold Machin to restore some of the lost grandeur with his definitive set.

But if one has some reservations about the low value definitives, one can have none about Lynton Lamb's high value Castles issue (see p. 14) which appeared in 1955. A handsome set in every way and not wholly ruined by the romantic stone embrasure and carefully placed weeds which, much against his better judgement, he was obliged to include. The dies for the portrait and the landscapes were engraved by Waterlow's engraver, Mr Bard, from the Dorothy Wilding photograph and from Lynton Lamb's own watercolours. The Post Office had initially proposed to print the stamps in two colours, but fortunately Lynton Lamb and Waterlows persuaded them to keep to a single printing.

It is the Coronation issue of 1953 that heralds a new era of stamp design, for here is the first example for nearly twenty years of the move towards a more graphic design solution, comparable to the magnificent Silver Jubilee issue by Barnett Freedman of 1935. Once again the COID Committee and the Postmaster General's Advisory Panel had fallen into the old trap of not being able to make up their mind on one design only. Maybe the choice was a conscious one, in an attempt to give variety to the set, but it is difficult to understand why they did not go for Edmund Dulac's 1s 3d design and

7/4 The Coronation issue of 1953: a more graphic solution

print it in four colourways. Then it might well have been one of the best issues of the reign. Even so, E. C. Fuller's 2½d, Michael Goarman's 4d and Edmund Dulac's 1s 3d are all magnificent stamps, with the first prize going to Dulac for a quite unmistakable statement. Of all the four his is the one that immediately says 'Coronation.'

It is interesting that, instead of using the Dorothy Wilding portrait, Dulac asked to be allowed to make his own full face portrait so that he could then show the Queen in her Coronation robes. A brilliant touch.

Misha Black OBE, FSIA, writing on the Coronation stamps in *Penrose Annual*, 1954, made an interesting point.

'The accelerating improvement in Government-controlled design has properly caused the critics successively to raise their sights so that they can continue to compare the present with an always equally distant future or with a persistently receding past. For the postage stamps the betterment is so apparent that the retreat of a hundred years can alone provide a suitable standard against which to judge the present issue.

The 1953 Coronation stamps are clearly the most satisfactory produced in Great Britain this side of 1900, with the possible exception of Eric Gill's 1938 issue.

It is a major revolution that Government printing should now be in the forward ranks instead of trailing miserably behind, as it did in the 'twenties and 'thirties. Great Britain alone issues stamps without the name of the country appearing in the design. The Coronation stamps do not shame this proud privilege.'

Compared with the 1960s, the rate of special stamp production was reasonably leisurely, for nothing appeared until the World Scout Jubilee Jamboree in 1957. Not a very distinguished set except perhaps for Mary Adshead's well controlled and organized 2½d. This issue was followed, one month later, by a single stamp issue for the 40th Inter-Parliamentary Union Conference which must rank as the worst stamp of the reign. One can hear all the arguments being advanced by the Post Office that there was no time to do anything else but adapt the 4d definitive, but it is difficult to believe that this abomination was the best that they and Harrisons could achieve. It is some consolation that it is quite impossible to find another stamp, during twenty-five years of issues, quite so bad (see p. 80).

One of the limiting factors in the design of Commemorative or special issues of stamps was the Post Office requirement that the Sovereign's head must be the dominant element in the design and that it must be reproduced in a size no smaller than that on the definitive stamps. The effect therefore

7/5,6 The 1957 World Scout
Jubilee Jamboree, followed by
the arguably worst stamp of the
reign (*below*)

was inevitably to force the designer to find a formal, more heraldic
solution. Although permission was given to reduce the head slightly over
the next fifteen years, it was not possible for designers to integrate the head
successfully until Arnold Machin produced his new definitive issue in 1967.

The use of symbolic elements was commonplace, indeed it was normally
specified in the Post Office brief. The British Empire and Commonwealth
Games issue of 1958 and a similar issue for the Commonwealth Games of
1970 demonstrate very clearly how Post Office thinking and designers'
attitudes had changed over the intervening twelve years.

In 1958, as the Games were to be held in Cardiff, the brief asked for
the inclusion of design elements symbolising Wales – preferably using the
Welsh dragon. In 1970, the brief to the designer was to make the design
illustrative of the games themselves and if possible, to stress the multi-racial
character of the events. The fact that they were to be held in Edinburgh did
not seem to be of great significance, other than that it should be stated in
the caption. As a pictorial issue Andrew Restall's designs of 1970 are well in
advance of the very mixed 1958 set.

Over the next few years a very distinctive style was beginning to emerge,
a style which had the marks of the designer rather than the artist. Faith

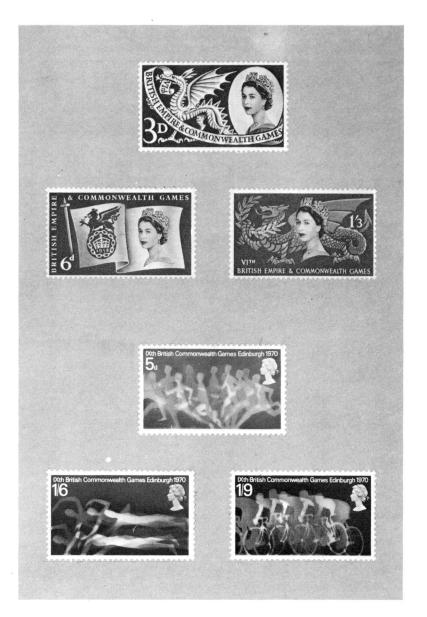

7/7,8 The British Empire and
Commonwealth Games issue of
1958 compared with the 1970
issue for the Commonwealth
Games

Jaques' 'General Letter Office' 1s 3d, Peter Gauld's 2½d and Michael and Sylvia Goaman's 1s 6d – both in the 'Savings Bank Centenary' issue – and the Goamans 'Freedom from Hunger,' were all controlled and well-organized designs. Also the concept of a unified issue was beginning to become established even though there were some oddities which are difficult to justify, like the 2s 6d intrusion into David Gentleman's Shakespeare set – good as Robin and Christopher Ironside's line-engraved stamp is. Quite clearly philatelic considerations took precedence over design logic. Half-a-crown came into the high value range and high value stamps by tradition were printed by this process. Therefore, whatever the photogravure values looked like, the line-engraved value could not possibly be *en suite*. And exactly the same thing happened in 1966 in the Westminster Abbey set. Such a pity, for they are both very good stamps individually, but cannot possibly make a good pair.

7/9,10,11,12 Faith Jaques' 1s 3d, Peter Gauld's 2½d, Michael and Sylvia Goaman's 1s 6d and (*below*) their 'Freedom from Hunger' set: well organized designs

7/13 The Shakespeare set: four stamps by David Gentleman and the 2s 6d intruder by Robin and Christopher Ironside

7/14 The Westminster Abbey set: photogravure for the low value against line-engraving for the high value

There is a nice story on this question of consistency which relates to the
Churchill issue of 1965 (see p. 68). The COID Advisory Panel could not
make up its mind between a set by David Gentleman and one by Abram
Games. So, rather unwisely, it recommended to the Queen the issue of two
stamps – one from each designer. The Queen, God Bless Her, decided
otherwise, preferring consistency to inconsistency and by choosing the
Gentleman pair she gave her approval to one of the most distinguished
stamp issues of her reign. In fairness though, Abram Games's design was
most adventurous and a pair of them would have made an equally good
set. But to pursue this a stage further. To my mind this issue embodies all
the attributes of total graphic communication. The message is loud and
clear without the use of explanatory words. All three operational requirements are expressed in graphic terms. Nearly the perfect stamp and the
descendant of the first ever, the Penny Black, and equal to Dulac's Coronation stamp.

It is perhaps this quality of intellectual analysis, expressed in a highly
professional design manner that distinguishes between a good and not so
good design solution. David Gentleman has only equalled this performance in three other issues: his Battle of Britain set later in the same year
(see p. 61), the three stamps related to Caernarvon Castle in the Investiture issue of 1969, and the Social Reformers issue in 1976 (see p. 118–19).

But look again at the Battle of Britain issue. Never before had a story
been told on a set of stamps with such economy of design expression and
with such a condensation of visual communication. Accept that there are
only two stamps which tell the whole story, the one showing the swastika-
marked aircraft being ditched by four Spitfires and the black cross wing
being obliterated by the RAF roundel – maybe elsewhere this symbolism
could be read another way, but for us it is crystal clear. The remaining four
individual designs only make sense in terms of these two. But this is a
typical Gentleman trick and where he has been able to persuade the Post
Office to play it, it has been most successful, if a little expensive in fees.
What is disappointing in this issue is that Andrew Restall's 9d design is very
much the odd man out. We know that rather late in the day the ground
forces had asked to be included, quite properly, and Andrew's design was
the only one which filled the bill. But with David himself breaking his own
unsquared-up pattern for one design out of seven, it seems odd that no
compromise could have been reached to bring Andrew Restall's design
into conformity with the remainder of the issue. All it needed was the same
treatment of the Queen's portrait and the value numerals as appeared in
David Gentleman's designs. A small, if not minor, point, maybe, but one

7/15 Battle of Britain: Andrew
Restall's and David
Gentleman's stamps which
break the design of the set as a
whole (*below*)

7/17 Three stamps from the
1967 British Flora issue: the
drawings are similar in style,
the treatment is different
(*opposite*)

7/16 David Gentleman's
Caernarvon Castle stamps for
the Investiture issue of 1969

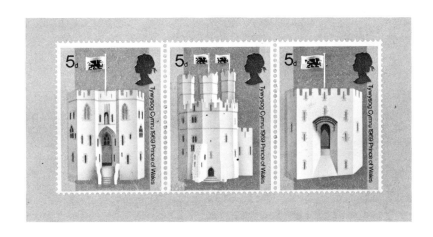

which demonstrates the need for somebody somewhere to have been aware
that it is attention to such minutiae of design which in the end produces the
best result.

On the same theme it would have been but a short step to achieve a
consistent and unified design for the British Flora issue of 1967. The
drawings of the Rev. Keble Martin and Mary Grierson are so similar in
style as to make the difference in treatment of the Queen's head and value
numerals quite unnecessary. Once again, I doubt whether there was
anyone at the time in a position of authority to see what little was needed to
make this into an extremely good set. As it is, in spite of Mary Grierson's
most sensitive drawing, the typographical treatment is so heavy-handed as
to let down the whole issue.

7/17 Three stamps from the
1967 British Flora issue: the
drawings are similar in style,
the treatment is different

Chronologically this may be the appropriate place to start looking at the long string of painting reproductions, for July 1967 saw the first issue of just such stamps which were to recur over the next twelve years. This type of issue had long been under discussion in the COID, with the result that at a meeting of the Advisory Committee it was agreed that the following paintings should be recommended to the Postmaster General, from which he could make his own choice for the three stamps he proposed to issue.

George Stubbs	*William Anderson, a groom with two horses*;
	Lady and Gentleman in a carriage;
William Hogarth	*The Shrimp Girl*;
John Constable	*The Haywain*;
J. M. W. Turner	*Peace: Burial at Sea*;
	The Fighting Temeraire;
Gainsborough	*Mrs Siddons*;
	The Artist's two Children;
Millais	*The Blind Girl*;

MacTaggart, Alan Ramsay, Nicholas Hillyard, although no paintings were specified.

It had been suggested that a painting by L. S. Lowry should be in the set, as it was understood that this painter was favoured by the then Prime Minister. The Panel, however, had advised against work by a living painter. The set finally issued was *Master Lambton* by Sir Thomas Lawrence, *Mares and Foals in a Landscape* by George Stubbs and *Children coming out of School* by L. S. Lowry. Not one of these paintings had been recommended by the Advisory Committee.

7/18 The controversial paintings issue of 1967

I was then Typographic Adviser to the Postmaster General, on a part-time basis, and I was asked to recommend the treatment of the Queen's head and the value denomination. I was far from satisfied with the result, in so far as the mixture of size and format made an untidy set.

When I was asked to do the same thing with the Christmas issue for the same year, in no way could I find a solution to the Le Nain *Adoration* than by breaking UPU rules and spelling out the value across the foot of the stamp. The fact that the painting had a donkey's head on one side and a cow's rump on the other, made the positioning of the Sovereign's effigy a rather more than normally sensitive problem.

7/19 Christmas 1967: the Le Nain Adoration with the value spelt out

Yet another issue of reproductions, in August of the following year, made me question the whole design approach to such issues, if indeed one could describe this sort of contriving as design. I suggested to the Postmaster General that the haphazard placing of the Queen's head and value numeral on the reproduction was perhaps not the best way to arrive at a satisfactory result. Maybe we should keep these two elements clear of the painting image. But no, I had to make the painting fill the space. At least I was able to devise a standard relationship between the Queen's head and the value, even though they were both barely legible.

By now I had come firmly to the conclusion that this was not the best way to design stamps, unless it was impracticable to find an alternative solution. This was the case with the next four issues of reproductions, Ulster Paintings in 1971, Reynolds and Raeburn in 1973, Turner in 1975 and Horseracing in 1979. So apologetic did I feel about this approach that I could not bring myself to ask another designer to arrange the issues, so I did them myself.

7/20 The paintings issue of 1968, a design compromise which was better resolved in the next four issues (see next page)

7/21 The Ulster paintings of
1971, the Reynolds and
Raeburn issue of 1973, the
Turner one of 1975

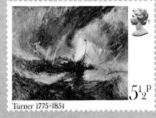

With the Ulster set, the political situation was beginning to become so sensitive that, having tried all sorts of pictorial ideas of a promotional nature, we decided to go for as non-controversial an issue as possible. If one accepts the need to produce this kind of stamp, then I believe the Ulster set is the most satisfying one we produced. I was determined at least to keep the Queen's head, numerals and caption off the reproduction, mainly encouraged by Anthony Lousada's criticism in the Stamps Advisory Committee of the Constable *Haywain* on this very score.

I spent a long time in Northern Ireland trying to find the right paintings and those small enough, so as not to suffer overmuch by reduction. I was greatly helped by the Arts Council of Northern Ireland which was itself planning exhibitions of Ulster painters for the 1971 Festival. As with all these paintings issues, I made no final choice until George York of Harrisons had appraised the original from a printing point of view.

Given the need to commemorate Sir Joshua Reynolds and Sir Henry Raeburn, both of whom had anniversaries in 1973, what else could the Post Office do but reproduce their work? I was very anxious to take a detail of some of their paintings, preferably portraits, and indeed prepared a set of

7/22 The horseracing stamps of 1979

designs on that basis. But when we came to Sir Joshua's self-portrait, now
in Burlington House, which really we could not ignore, it was made quite
clear to me that we would only get the President of the Royal Academy's
permission to reproduce it if we included the whole painting. A pity really,
because it is nearly eight foot tall!

When we came to Turner, two years later, we were in much the same
trouble, for we felt obliged to reproduce both his oils and his watercolours,
and some of the more attractive oils are very large. In a funny way I quite
liked the loss of definable detail. The stamps almost became abstractions of
the paintings, rather like the Ulster paintings, and they took on a quality of
their own. But I cannot honestly be proud of these stamps, for they seem to
me to lack the essential quality by which the graphic expression of an
intellectual solution succeeds in terms of design and production. The best a

7/23,24,25,26 The better use of
reproductions: Rosalind Dease's
Inigo Jones, and (*on the right*)
Richard Gay's Caxton, Sally
Stiff's de Lisle Psalter, and
another Dease: Dickens as seen
by Cruikshank

William Caxton 1476   8½ᴾ

William Caxton 1476   10ᴾ

William Caxton 1476   11ᴾ

William Caxton 1476   13ᴾ

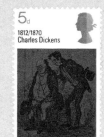

printer can do with this type of subject is to interpret it. He cannot physically reproduce it, even though his interpretation of all these issues has been masterly.

On the other hand, there are one or two exceptions to this rule which may sustain the practice of reproduction – or shall we say re-use. Rosalind Dease's issue for Inigo Jones turns his drawings into the dominant element in her designs. And quite properly, for these drawings were the means by which the masque costumes were made, the Covent Garden church was built or the Court Masque scenery was painted. They were not made to be seen as works of art in their own right as are paintings or drawings. In much the same way I would justify Richard Gay's use of the Caxton book-engravings, Sally Stiff's de Lisle Psalter illuminations for Christmas 1970 and Rosalind Dease's Cruikshank drawings for the Dickens issue of 1970.

8 Royal Mail design and the new Stamp Advisory Committee

One of the first steps Edward Short, the new Postmaster General, took was to disband the old COID Committee. In view of the new stamps-issuing programme announced by Wedgwood Benn some eighteen months previously and of the prospect of a new status in the shape of a public corporation, it was only natural that the Post Office should want rather more control on the design and production of stamps. Edward Short lost little time in setting up a new committee, with less emphasis on Establishment Art and more on design, philately and the common man (or woman).

Letters of invitation to serve on the committee were sent out on 12 December 1967, in which he wrote: 'I want this to be a body comprising experts in design, representatives of public opinion generally and philatelists. The broad terms of reference of the Committee will be 'to advise the Postmaster General on (a) the artists to be invited to submit designs for stamps, (b) the briefs according to which the artist will work, and (c) the designs to be submitted for Her Majesty's approval'. The Committee will be advisory in the sense that responsibility for final decisions on stamp design has to remain with me since stamps are issued in my name.'

All those asked to serve accepted the Postmaster General's invitation and the new Committee met for the first time on Wednesday 21 February 1968. The members were: Brian Batsford, MP, Conservative member for Ealing South; Kenneth Chapman, Editor *Stamp Collecting*; Richard Guyatt, FSIA, ARCA, Professor of Graphic Design at the Royal College of Art; R. A. G. Lee, Fellow and Council Member of the Royal Philatelic Society; Anthony Lousada, Solicitor, and Chairman of the Trustees of the Tate Gallery; Mrs Louise Pearce, housewife and one time organizer of the National Association of Women's Clubs; Sir Paul Reilly, Director of the Council of Industrial Design; George Rogers, CBE, MP, Labour Member for North Kensington; Stuart Rose, FSIA, Typographic Adviser to the Postmaster General; and Herbert Spencer, RDI, FSIA, graphic designer. The Chairman was George Downes, CB, Director, Operations and Overseas Department of the Post Office, an able and experienced Civil Servant who for a period after the war was seconded to the Cabinet Office as Principal Private Secretary to a succession of Ministers. The Secretary was J. R. Baxter, an Assistant Secretary in the Department which also administered the Committee. The Committee was also attended by George York, OBE, Works Director of Harrison & Sons (High Wycombe) Ltd, the stamp printers, who advised on technical matters relating to the particular stamps they were printing. The other printers concerned sent their own representatives as the occasion demanded. The Committee had been appointed in the first instance for a term of three years.

The setting up of this Committee was perhaps the most important step that had been taken in the long history of stamp production, for it established for the first time the Post Office's own self-sufficiency in the complete control of stamp production. Never before had it been in the position to exercise its own expert judgement in an area of Post Office activity which for the past century and a quarter had often been over-whelmed with outside advice. Here at last was an opportunity for the Post Office to speak with a rather more authoritative voice.

In accordance with the same policy of greater Post Office involvement in design, the post of Design Director was created a few months later by Alan Wolstencroft, then Deputy Director-General; I was invited to fill it, and thus became a full-time member of Post Office staff in November 1968, with a notional responsibility for design throughout the Postal business.

Very soon the stamps programme began to claim more and more of my time. The most significant difference in the procedures, which were fol-lowed under the old Committee structure and now under the new one, was the increased involvement of the Stamps Division with designers. Their commissioning was now firmly in Post Office hands, for I had the firm conviction that the best way to secure high standards of design and production was to establish the closest working relationship between the client, the designer and the manufacturer.

None of this would have been possible without the very close re-lationship we were building up with Harrisons, especially through George York, the High Wycombe Works Director. The change in stamp issuing policy had created a wholly new situation between the Post Office and the printers with the Department of Operations and Overseas gradually assuming responsibility for printer/Post Office liaison previously enjoyed by the Supplies Department.

The printer began to play a different role from that of being the contractor who only had to maintain a regular and adequate supply of definitive stamps. His contribution to the interpretation and reproduction of the designs was of far greater significance than his function as 'con-tractor' would seem to demand. This new relationship, not being on a client/contractor basis, enabled the designer and the Post Office to identify with the printer to the point where the line of demarcation between client and supplier disappeared. Between us we had one job to do, to produce the best possible stamps that time and circumstance would allow; and it was the unquestioning acceptance of this common objective that made it possible for us all to produce some quite outstanding results. Essential to this attitude was a determination on the printer's part that nothing short of perfection in the reproduction and interpretation of the designer's work was good enough and he would go to endless lengths to see that it was so.

And, of course, the Works Staff accepted this kind of challenge in a way that on most occasions was quite remarkable. I well remember the way in which they reacted to Marjorie Saynor's 'Explorers' and Barbara Brown's 'Jane Austen'; for both sets of stamps had been drawn at stamp size, instead of four times enlarged which was normal practice. Therefore the job of reproduction was made far more difficult as there was not the same room to manoeuvre. The reproductions had to be exactly as the originals. But, being craftsmen themselves, they had an appreciation for the great skill that had created the miniature paintings and they responded to it.

Perhaps it was because I had worked for a number of years as a designer in a printing firm that I felt at home with the printers. We knew and understood each other's problems, so that there was a measure of mutual respect in our working relationship.

A pattern of work very quickly established itself. The Executive Officer responsible for the day-to-day running of the programme in the Department was Don Beaumont, a dedicated and lovable cynic and soon to become a very real friend. Together we would decide who were the best designers to commission for a particular issue; we retained the old form of commissioning them first through the post, but always arranging a meeting between the three of us before they got too deeply involved in the design problems. Ultimately the postal brief gave way to a phone call asking a designer to come to my office for a preliminary talk. I preferred that way because it enabled all of us to start thinking aloud about an issue, before we became too set in our ideas. Depending on the complexity of the subject, these meetings would recur right up until the time when we were all satisfied that a design had been sufficiently developed and refined to put to the Committee. We would then be joined by George York, so that we could all be aware of any production problems inherent in the designs.

In the background we had the support of Jerry Baxter and the Director, George Downes, who allowed us remarkable freedom to pursue a very stringent design policy. I regard those years certainly as the most productive in my short time in Postal Headquarters, largely, I believe, because all of us were conscious of the need to establish a pattern of performance professionally outstanding in design and production.

The whole exercise was expanding all the time. Soon, round about early 1969, we were beginning to apply the same design standards to all the supporting printed material that accompanies a stamp issue – First Day Covers, presentation packs and the like – and gradually we were creating precedents which we hoped would be the norm below which future production should not be allowed to fall.

It took quite a long time, nevertheless, for these single-minded attitudes to seep through the whole system. Although the Committee on the whole was sympathetic to what we were striving to do, at times it would rather perversely try to express its own personal opinion rather than judgement.

Except for one or two designer members, I do not believe that the rest of the Committee understood the measure of our involvement in this communal act of design direction. From the first moment of commissioning a designer there was established a very close professional relationship, at first between the designer and ourselves at the Post Office then gradually involving the printers through George York. Always working to the designer's pace we would have as many meetings and discussions as we all thought essential to enable us to arrive at a design solution which we were satisfied met the design requirements of the problem – both political and aesthetic. Only then would the designs be put to the Committee supported on occasion by the presence of the designer who made the presentation.

It was the intensity and depth of this progression of design involvement, which we all knew to be an essential part of the design function, that made me increasingly intolerant of some of the Committee comments. They had not been through the detailed analytical process of design development that we had undertaken and I resented what I considered to be amateur interference with a highly considered professional design solution. No wonder that one Committee member accused me of allowing my spleen to infect my blood stream!

A life time career both of designing and design direction leaves me in no doubt whatsoever that good industrial design can only emerge from the kind of tri-partite relationship which we were all trying to establish between the client, the designer and the manufacturer and very rarely results from Committee procedures, however well intentioned.

I was talking to David Gentleman about the whole question of designers getting involved with Committees and I asked him what his view was.

DG: 'I believe that the ideal client is an intelligent and well-disposed despot and therefore working through a Committee brings certain kinds of problems with it. I can remember the Stamps Advisory Committee as being a nice and amiable one and the only serious difficulty is that, if you are not careful, you can be persuaded to do something for the sake of good nature, rather than because it is the best thing to do. It could be that one persuasive individual, rather than the Committee itself, could put you in that position. I have always regretted that I allowed myself to be over-persuaded on the BBC issue to bring TV into the set. The argument put forward was that TV was too important to ignore, but it had nothing to do with the reason for the issue, which was to commemorate fifty years of continuous public radio broadcasting. I am still very proud of the loud-speaker horn design and there was no good reason why the other stamps should not have been period relics like that one.'

I asked Philip Sharland how he reacted, when he was designing stamps, to having a Committee in the background. Did it worry him at all?

PS: 'I hated it. The judgement of twelve good men and true, or whatever, is so subjective. I have not seen the Committee in action, but I would have thought that there would be a lot of point-making for personal reasons, not really objective, sensible or informed comment. That kind of opinion inevitably arrives at some sort of compromise, however you try to guide it.'

SR: 'I don't think you and I suffered unduly with the stamps that you were doing.'

PS: 'But do you really think that this is the right way to arrive at a good solution?'

SR: 'No, I don't, not a design solution. I do think it is sensible, though, for the Post Office to have available a group of people to advise on policy and, in fact, to bring a deal of outside experience and a varied point of view to bear on questions which can become rather inbred. Also it can be a warm overcoat for the Post Office against the cold winds of public criticism.'

PS: 'Is it not too big?'

SR: 'Certainly, if you look at it as a "design" committee. A meeting of a dozen people is too big to allow for the intimate exchange of experience and judgement, which is at the heart of any serious discussion on design. But if you see it as a committee to advise on policy, then it isn't too big, because it represents a very wide span of relevant interests and can be of immense benefit to the Post Office.'

There is, of course, an inherent deficiency built into a body such as this Committee, in its quite natural inability to remember from one meeting to another, with any degree of accuracy, what it had decided to do. With the result that actions, which we the secretariat had taken following Committee decisions at one meeting, would be questioned – if not counter-manded – at the next.

I must confess that once the euphoria of the early years was starting to wear off, I began to get more and more disillusioned by the whole system of Committee advice. It seemed to me that as a body it didn't possess the necessary professional expertise to add anything of value to what the secretariat, the designer and the printer had already decided; and its

8/1 The 1968 Christmas issue

comment was beginning to become disruptive, so that already I was having to build a defence mechanism to protect first the designer and then the position taken up by the Post Office. I found it disturbing, particularly when I felt convinced that the opportunity to involve all those dedicated people in the wider issues of stamp production was being allowed to slip.

Yet when you look at what had been published since the Committee was first set up, the record is not unimpressive. The first issues it was concerned with were the Anniversaries set of May 1968 (TUC, Votes for Women, Captain Cook, and the RAF), the paintings issue of August 1968 and the Christmas Children's Games set. On none of these issues could it make much impact, for the designs were well down the production road by the time it first met.

After that, the Ships issue is commendable, while Concorde is not; far too many mixed design metaphors. The 1969 Anniversaries was a disaster in design control, the Cathedrals were good, and the Investiture (see also p. 85) was masterly in all but two stamps – the portrait and the Margam Abbey Cross.

But these two stamps exemplify the risks of listening too closely to outside advice. The Welsh naturally wanted us to be Welshly patriotic and show something sufficiently old to be uncontroversial, whilst everyone else thought we should have a portrait of the Prince himself. All laudable motifs, but in the event they robbed the set of the greater distinction which it would have maintained had we kept to David Gentleman's concept of the Fairyland Castle. The whole event had a touch of make-believe about it and David captured that atmosphere brilliantly.

There's a nice story on this particular point of official advice. We had been told to steer clear of one particular element of heraldry, which we did assiduously.

It so happened that I had been seeing the Controller of the Ministry of Public Buildings and Works on the question of furniture and furnishings for the Post Office, with the result that he sent me an invitation to the Press Preview of the decor for Caernarvon Castle, held in the MPBW building in Endell Street.

I suggested to George Downes that we might go together and see how our stamps would compare with the official stage settings.

Imagine our dismay on entering the exhibition to find the proscribed heraldic device on everything! Once we had recovered from our fury at being so wrongly informed, we came to the conclusion that we were lucky not to have fallen into the obvious trap. At least our stamps were totally different from anything else to do with the celebration.

8/2,3,4 The Ships set of 1969, the Cathedrals of the same year, and the two odd stamps in the Investiture set

The only disappointment with this otherwise quite lovely set was the effect the phosphor had on the metallic background. I suppose we should have realized that when we agreed to David's idea of silver instead of colour, but by then it was too late to change. Incidentally this was the first issue on which we had used a metallic colour.

In 1971 the Stamps Advisory Committee was reappointed for a further three years with two newcomers; Mrs Gabrielle Pike, CBE, JP, a past Chairman of the National Federation of Women's Institutes, replacing Mrs Louise Pearce; and Mr Eric Ogden, MP for Liverpool (West Derby) taking Mr George Rogers' place.

The year before had seen the issuing of the first Decimal Currency definitives. For many months before we had been working very closely with Dr I. D. Brown, the Post Office physiological consultant, at the Medical Research Council in Cambridge, to try to arrive at a practical range of colours for the new decimal range. The original set of definitives had been overtaken by operational events which had laid bare certain deficiencies in the choice of colours. It should be remembered that within the definitive range of 18 stamps produced in 1953 there were 5 different designs, so that value recognition relied as much on the difference of pattern as on colour. In the 1967 issue of definitives however, the design content was constant throughout the set, thereby making value recognition by colour far more significant, particularly in the case of mechanical sorting.

Arnold Machin's new definitive designs in 1967 had been based on a very clear aesthetic formula, the portrayal of the Sovereign's head in light tonal relief against a dark background. We managed to get by operationally with most of the colours but when, in 1968, the two-tier system was introduced the distinction between the two colours representing the two classes of service (4d brown and 5d blue) was not clear enough either for manual or mechanical sorting. The most satisfactory stamp aesthetically, the brown 4d, was the least successful operationally. So it was replaced by the new red 4d which made the right contrast with the blue 5d.

So with the prospect of a wholly new definitive issue, due for publication in 1970 on the introduction of decimal currency, some very serious thought had to be given to the colour range. We considered these factors:

1. The need to choose colours for the more popular values which would be visually distinctive for manual sorting and
2. the need to ensure that those same colours would give an acceptable signal when sorted mechanically.

3. The advantage of arranging the value order of the colours in such a way that pairs of colours in single step values, representing first and second class mail, would be distinguishable whatever the future increases in tariffs might be.
4. And lastly, to make them as aesthetically satisfying as operational demands would allow.

We had already been able to plot the sterling colour range in order of signal strength, but more information was wanted over a wider range of colours if we were to have a greater number of known positives from which to choose the fourteen stamps necessary for the issue.

With the help of Harrisons, the printers, we proofed up something like 40 colour variants and they were subjected to electronic tests by our engineers, who weeded out those colours which did not give an acceptable signal. We ended up with a range of 25 possible colours.

These proofs we then sent to the Applied Psychology Research Unit of the Medical Research Council at Cambridge where Dr I. D. Brown conducted a series of 'confusability' tests by the method of paired comparisons. Each of the 25 colours was paired with itself and with the other 24 in the range and the two colours in each pair were displayed successively. Members of the panel were asked to state whether the two specimens of each pair were the same or different from one another and to indicate the confidence with which they reached their conclusions.

The results from the tests were plotted to give a rank order of confusability plus confidence which gave us a range of 14 colours which were acceptable within tolerable limits. A second test was carried out, after Arnold Machin had made a few amendments, before a panel this time of 26 housewives and 10 postmen. Surprisingly the results showed a striking similarity in judgement between the professional postmen and the amateur housewife.

Dr Brown had built his theory on half the range being a set of seven full strength colours, the remaining seven being lighter tones of the first group. In Dr Brown's view, the degree of memorability of colours exposed for a minimal period, is in direct relation to the ability one has to express colours to oneself in literary terms. Any hesitancy, therefore, in describing mentally in words a colour that is seen, will reduce the recall factor when this same colour is next seen.

The experiment proved extremely successful, although with hindsight I believe we should have involved Arnold Machin rather earlier in helping us to make the original selection of colours. On the whole the final range

behaved most efficiently, even though we could have improved the aesthetic quality of some values without prejudicing their operational
effectiveness. During 1971 I was also allowed to create the post of Design
Co-ordinator. There was no question that the right man to fill it was Peter
Shrives, a one-time designer and technical illustrator, who for the past
three years had been Deputy Publicity Manager, Postal Headquarters.
We had worked together since 1962, when I was doing a considerable
amount of free-lance designing for the Public Relations Department,
where he was then placed. His arrival took a considerable load off me and,
indeed, was the beginning of a most fruitful, successful and enjoyable
association, laying the foundations of a very active Design Division, which
he now leads. Without question, those few years were perhaps the most
frustrating for both of us, but certainly the most exciting, because they gave
us the tremendous satisfaction of beginning to see results, however slowly.
Peter's main contribution was in directing and managing the design of the
supporting material for stamp issues, as well as being very closely involved
with me, Don Beaumont and George York on the stamps themselves.
Remember too, that stamps only occupied half our time.

8/5 The Royal Silver Wedding
stamps of 1972

It was the Royal Silver Wedding stamps of November 1972 which
demonstrated, more than any other issue so far, the value of the new
combined approach to design. Jeffery Matthews and Broome Lynne had
been commissioned in May 1971 to produce preliminary designs so that we
could get broad approval from the Palace on the general design approach
to the stamps. We very quickly decided on a photographic treatment
which Jeffery Matthews himself had recommended. One of the problems
he had to overcome was the fact that the stamps were commemorating the
Wedding of HRH Princess Elizabeth and HRH The Duke of Edinburgh
and not that of the Queen. Whereas they must have about them an
unmistakable sense of royalty, they should if possible, forego the pomp and
circumstance of Regality. Quite a different problem from that of the Silver
Jubilee and the Coronation which followed later. Jeffery Matthews managed to give his designs just that right balance of dignity, authority and
personality.

Although we looked at all the available photographs it soon became
apparent that new ones would have to be taken. The Palace approved and
Norman Parkinson was commissioned. It was George York who suggested
that we should use Norman Parkinson on the strength of the work he did
with Harrisons. He had recently taken a lovely series of photographs of
HRH Princess Anne for her 21st birthday, some of which Harrisons had
printed in a colour supplement for a national newspaper. In the event the

8/6 Princess Anne's Wedding issue with accepted designs and final artwork

new portraits were printed monochrome from colour originals. The risk of the slightest misregister of any of the colour plates at stamp size, and the inevitable distortion that would follow, persuaded us against full colour reproduction.

Jeffery Matthews also designed the First Day Covers, so that for the first time we were able to submit to the Palace both values of stamps essayed in a variety of colours and mounted as pairs on proofs of the covers.

While on the subject of royal portraits, perhaps it is appropriate to mention the next wedding event: that of HRH Princess Anne and Captain Mark Phillips in November 1973. Following so soon after her parents' Silver Wedding it seemed important to us that this stamp should in no way be seen to imitate, in design terms, the issue of the previous year. Yet in many respects the problem was comparable.

But if the question of design was likely to prove difficult, that of their production, at first sight, seemed insurmountable. The Engagement was announced on 29 May and the stamps would have to be issued on 14 November. The real problem, having decided that new photographs

would have to be taken, was to find an opportunity for Lord Lichfield, whom the Princess had recommended, to photograph the couple together. Captain Mark Phillips was in Germany with his regiment and there seemed no chance of him returning in time, so we arranged for Patrick Lichfield to go to Germany and photograph Mark Phillips alone. But our luck held. A telephone call from the Palace told us that the Princess and the Captain would both be at Hickstead on Sunday 22 July, returning to Windsor that evening. Frantic last minute arrangements with Patrick Lichfield to get him to the Castle in time for the helicopter. He took three or four reels in the grounds, they were processed that night and in the hands of the designer on Monday afternoon.

This quite frightening programme could never have been kept, had we not had the greatest possible help from the Palace, and especially from Princess Anne's office, as well as from Patrick Lichfield, to say nothing of the quite remarkable production achievements at High Wycombe.

Not surprisingly, we had to dispense with much of the formal procedures that normally attend an issue. There just was not the time to go back to the Committee for its agreement to each step we were taking. We just did it and backed our own judgement. Fortunately George White, the Chairman of the Committee, supported us. The crucial issue was that the stamps should be available on 14 November. And they were.

Ironically it was Patrick Lichfield's great-great-grandfather who, as Postmaster General in 1837, so strongly opposed Rowland Hill's reform. We all agreed that it was just as well that his opposition had proved fruitless, even though he may have turned in his grave at our antics!

We had another nice problem in June of the following year, the Centenary of the Universal Postal Union. The designs by Rosalind Dease, which we ultimately used, show quite distinctly the great change that had overtaken commemorative issues since, say, the first UPU stamps in 1929. No other issue, I believe, states so clearly the fundamental shift in Post Office policy. There is nothing in that issue which even attempts to explain graphically what the Universal Postal Union was all about; and I suppose if one is sympathetic to the label argument then there is no good reason why you should enjoy Rosalind Dease's solution. But on the way between these two extremes, particularly from the very astringent John Farleigh $\frac{1}{2}$d and $2\frac{1}{2}$d and the Nelson £1 value, take a look at the same subject as portrayed in 1949 (see p. 41) and then decide whether the Rosalind Dease set of 1974 is not much closer to the contemporary design idiom.

That same year also saw the publication of a remarkable set of Great Britons by Fritz Wegner, an issue bedevilled by a quite extraordinary display of political nervousness. It all started with Robert the Bruce who that year, 1974, was celebrating his 700th birthday. Surely the occasion for a commemorative stamp. But the Scots wanted to include Wallace as well. The precedent had already been established that given one national subject in an issue, there should if possible be three more comparable subjects representing as it were the remaining three parts of the United Kingdom. For Scotland to field two candidates seemed a little greedy. Owain Glyndower seemed a natural and reasonable contemporary, as did the Black Prince. Then somehow Boadicea joined the act; quite out of period and graphically she would create so many problems of consistency, as she would only be recognizable in her chariot and that would mean a horse or two. Fortunately, further researches indicated that she was always driven by a charioteer and that he was always naked! Whether it was the appreciation of the design problem of accommodating two figures and two horses within the small confines of a stamp or the fear of an accusation of indelicacy that finally persuaded the Committee Chairman I do not know, but Boadicea was out. As also was the next on the list, Edward I, the Hammer of the Scots of whom our advisors said, in all seriousness, that his inclusion in the issue would be politically unacceptable to the Scots.

8/7 The Universal Postal Union stamps of 1974 by Rosalind Dease

Edward had planned the conquest of Scotland in 1294 and never achieved it! But even more surprisingly, the Post Office accepted the objection and replaced him with Henry V. There were times when it was impossible for the Post Office not to find itself in this sort of ridiculous situation, but equally there were times when its reaction should really have been a long, loud laugh.

Even so, that issue still stands as one of the most glamorous of the period and is a wonderful example of the synthesis of impeccable illustration and controlled disposition of all the parts that is the essence of good design. Without question a great deal of the success of this issue is due to the unfailing support we all had from the College of Heralds. They were unstinting in the advice they gave Fritz Wegner and in the time they spent to check every detail of his drawings. So too was the Master of the Armouries, A. R. Dufty, at the Tower of London. They all thoroughly enjoyed this sort of involvement at a very high professional level, and it created a relationship which later was to prove of inestimable value.

Over the next two or three years there followed a succession of issues which established the Post Office as a thoroughly professional design organization. What I particularly like about this period is the variety of design solutions, as much as the very high technical skills of the designers themselves. From Jerczy Karo's 'Chemistry' to Barbara Brown's 'Jane Austen' or Ted Ripley's 'Cricket' to Nicholas Jenkins' 'University Buildings' (p. 108) and Richard Downer's variation on the Parliamentary theme (p. 109). Our Labour MP Committee member was furious when he realized that the House of Commons had been printed in blue with a Labour administration in power.

But for a totally different reason it was the Caxton issue that gave one most satisfaction. In 1971 the Post Office had offered the Royal Society of Arts a Postage Stamp Bursary to be included in its Industrial Design Student Bursary scheme. For a number of years the Post Office had

8/8 Fritz Wegner's Great Britons (stamps and sketches) of 1974

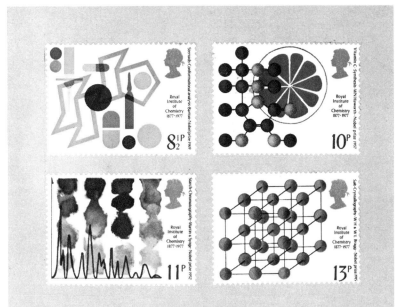

8/9,10,11 The successful issues:
Jerczy Karo's Chemistry
(1977), Barbara Brown's Jane
Austen (1975), Ted Ripley's
Cricket (1973)

8/12 Nicholas Jenkins'
University buildings (1971)

subscribed to the categories of publicity, typography, applied photo-
graphy and laminated plastics, but this was the first time it had suggested a
separate bursary for stamps. The set subject was 'Industrial Archaeology'
because, as the brief said, the subject had generated a considerable amount
of local interest throughout the country; its varied nature could be expected to attract the figurative and non-figurative designer; it provided the
opportunity for intelligent research; and it might very well become the
subject for an actual issue of stamps.

The subject did prove very popular and attracted seventy-six submissions from twenty-nine colleges and schools. The standard of design was
remarkably high and showed an encouraging knowledge and understanding of contemporary stamp design.

Harrisons very generously printed the winning set of designs se-tenant
on the sheet to be bound into an article which I had written on the Bursary
for *Penrose Annual*. Some of these sheets were later to find their way on to the
philatelic market under a wholly erroneous and misleading description.

8/13 Richard Downer's Inter-
Parliamentary Conference
(1975)

8/14 The winning set of
Industrial Archaeology designs
produced for the 1971 RSA
Student Bursary

So successful had been that year's competition that the Post Office repeated its offer the following year and for several years later.

In 1973 the Jury set as the subject the 150th Anniversary of the opening of the Stockton and Darlington Railway, an issue of stamps the Post Office would be making in 1975. Generally the standard was not so high as in the first year, but we did take one set by Stephen Moore of Southend College of Technology for him to develop with a view to publication. He did a considerable amount of work on these designs, but in the end he just failed to make his original concept work throughout the issue.

The following year however we were more successful with the Caxton Anniversary, being able to issue a set (see also p. 91) that Richard Gay, from Southend School of Art and Design, had developed with us from his winning submission.

He had to change two illustrations; one of a woodcut of a medieval printing house because he had already included a similar illustration, and

the other was an alleged portrait of Caxton. We nearly made a nonsense of
that stamp for only by chance did I find out that in fact the portrait was not
of Caxton but of some 17th century mid-European emperor. I had been
asked to design a First Day Cover for the British Printing Industries
Federation in connexion with the Caxton celebration and Brian Coulton,
of Harrisons, who that year was President of the Federation, had asked me
to lunch with John Shepherd, Public Relations Officer and James Moran,
an eminent printing historian who was Chairman of the Federation's
Celebration Committee. As they were all old friends I thought I was safe in
letting them see colour prints of Richard Gay's stamps. And just as well I
did. With a whoop of delight Jim Moran pounced on the offending portrait
and it was promptly withdrawn.

Ever since the foundation of the Post Office Bursary, it had been my
ambition that one day we should issue a set of stamps designed by the
winner. To have achieved it just three days before I retired was for me a
complete justification of our belief in the RSA scheme. The Caxton stamps
were issued on Wednesday 29 September 1976.

But if the Caxton stamps at the time gave me a sense of personal pride,
the one that appeared on Saturday 2 October was quite overwhelming.
That day was my 65th birthday and I and my family had been invited to a
small dinner party at the Arts Club by some friends. This 'small' party in
effect turned out to be a gathering of some forty or more designers, printers
and suppliers, with whom I had worked for the past ten years, together
with their wives. Sir Hugh Casson was in the Chair.

The menu was a delight both gastronomically and calligraphically,
having been scribed by Jeffery Matthews. David Gentleman had designed
the stamp (see back flap of jacket) using photographs he had taken at our
home one summer evening. When I questioned him for the reason, he
mumbled something about an article!

But if that wasn't joy enough, what followed dinner was even more so. A
huge solander box was carried in, seeming to weigh a ton, and containing a
remarkable collection of original works: drawings, paintings, photographs,
witticisms of one kind or another and all done specially by the designers
who were present at the dinner. Not only does that box contain a unique
record of a professional relationship which, during my time at the Post
Office, had produced some quite outstanding design results, it also stands
as a permanent reminder of the friendships which that association had
fostered.

8/15 Richard Gay's submissions
for the Caxton issue

9 The case histories of four recent issues

The problems connected with the design and production of every issue of stamps vary according to a number of conditions which are rarely the same for each issue. Apart from the subject itself, which imposes its own particular limitation, political considerations, the way in which the Post Office sees its own responsibility to the subject, the preferences of the 'sponsoring' body, when there happens to be one, all will have an influence on Post Office attitudes and thereafter on the design solutions.

To explain more fully the extent to which these influences can affect the design I have chosen four recent issues which created totally different problems for the Post Office, the designer and the printer. The issues are Village Churches 1962, Sailing 1975, Social Reformers 1976 and, taken together, the Silver Jubilee of 1977 and the 25th Anniversary of the Coronation in 1978.

Village Churches 1962
The decision to issue a set of stamps on village churches was taken in pursuit of a very loose policy to demonstrate, through a series of issues, the varied nature of British architecture. The stamps in this issue were not related to any particular event nor did they commemorate any particular building, unlike those in the issue which coincided with European Architectural Heritage Year in 1975 and included one for St George's Chapel Windsor on its 900th birthday and one for the National Theatre on its opening.

The most important part of the design problem consisted in the choice of the particular churches, rather more than in the style of expression. We had agreed in Committee that, in general terms, the set should represent all those architectural styles which together make up the extremely rich pattern of British ecclesiastical architecture and it was acknowledged that to do so demanded intensive research.

I had known Ronald Maddox, and his architectural drawings, ever since I started to illustrate Telephone Directories, and just as I admired his work, I knew him also to be a tireless researcher and to have in his possession an almost unique set of architectural sketch books. He was therefore commissioned to design the set, having first made his own study and submitted his proposals for the choice of churches. Never had an issue of stamps been supported by such thorough research into the subject. First, he listed thirty or more churches, separated into broad periods of date, and which demonstrated a particular architectural style. The list was supported by notes on the architectural features of each church justifying its inclusion in the list.

Village churches

He then arranged this same selection into groups of four churches to make up six possible sets, each one covering much the same architectural periods. At the same time he made nearly forty stamp-sized drawings to show different pictorial compositions, as illustrating the church in its village environment or complete as a portrait on its own, or extracting the main architectural feature, such as the tower.

By the time he had finished his researches and preliminary designs, the weight of material was so great that I suggested to George Downes, the Chairman of the Stamps Advisory Committee, that Ronald Maddox himself should attend the next meeting of the Committee to present and speak on his own recommendations. In the past I had involved designers in meetings of the Committee to talk about their own designs and this had always proved a useful and satisfying experience, both for the Committee and the designer. But this was the first time the designer was being asked, as it were, to present his own brief for the issue. And it worked. The Committee, I think, was overwhelmed by the thoroughness of Maddox's studies as well as being enchanted by his designs.

I regard this issue as having made a major stylistic contribution to the very wide range of architectural stamps issued in that period, and as one of the more satisfactory resolutions of a major problem. To condense six or seven hundred years of ecclesiastical architecture into five little stamps is no mean feat and Ronald Maddox has good reason to be proud of his achievement.

9/1 Preliminary drawings (*below*) and the black and white roughs for the Village Churches issue (*above*). On the right, colour drawings and the final issue

113

Greensted-juxta-Ongar Essex

Earls Barton Northants

Letheringsett Norfolk

Helpringham Lincs

Huish Episcopi Somerset

Sailing

9/2 Some of the rough
preliminary drawings for the
Sailing issue

Sailing 1975

If the dominant problem in the Village Churches issue was to write a comprehensive brief, the challenge in the Sailing issue was to design to the limitations of printing by two processes in one run, a production technique that had not as yet been fully tested. Harrisons, the printers, had recently installed a new two-process printing machine, 'Gemini', which had seven gravure cylinders and one three-colour engraved cylinder. Although the gravure side of the plant had proved itself to be a wonderful printer (and one has only to compare the quality of reproduction of the Machin definitives with that from the old press to appreciate the difference), we had not had the chance to prove the efficiency of the engraved system. So with the prospect of an issue on Sailing and all the problems of printing the fine lines in the rigging by gravure, George York and I decided to try out the engraved unit.

I commissioned Andrew Restall as a designer who was well informed on printing techniques and was adventurous enough in his approach to design to be able to produce some innovatory, if not revolutionary, ideas.

The three of us spent many hours in sorting out what the machine could and could not do and in the end arrived at a reasonable design formula. The basic shape and pattern of the stamp would be designed in broad flat colour terms which would be printed in gravure; the detail which would be rendered in line would be printed by line-engraved recess. This would accommodate obvious parts of the design of rigging and the like and would also give movement to the sea areas by a series of cross-hatched lines. So we went to work and Andrew produced some most exciting, almost abstract, designs of a variety of sailing vessels.

Perhaps I should say that, through the good offices of Anthony Lousada, a member of the Stamps Committee and himself a keen sailor, Andrew and I had had some extremely valuable talks with the Secretary of the Royal Yachting Association – which celebrated its centenary that year – to the extent that we were able to determine those classes of boats which should be represented on the stamps. In fairness to the Secretary, he displayed, if I may say so, great magnanimity in accepting Andrew's designs and indeed in persuading his Committee to do likewise; for all along I felt that he was expecting mini-photographic pictures of yachting dramas in the Solent and elsewhere.

Progressively, as we got deeper into the production problems, we realized that there were still a lot of bugs in the system that had not been worked out. The first design idiom that had to be jettisoned was the overprint of one engraved colour on another. In no way could this be made

9/3 A stage further in the
preparation of drawings with,
below, two drawings showing the
development of the design to
allow for the line engraving
process. At the bottom, the final
issue

to work without one colour 'bleeding' into another. So Andrew re-drew
those sheets to allow one colour to stop short, on the same plane, of another
by a defined distance. That seemed to work, even though it was a long way
from his original concept.

Paradoxically, in the end, it was not the press which was found wanting,
but the plumbing! It is no secret that the wastage on this issue was above
average, hence the short-fall in supply of certain denominations of the
stamps. But the galling part of the exercise was that, whereas Harrisons
had got a machine that could print supremely well, they could not cope
with a wholly new problem of disposing of the washing-up effluent.

One of the problems facing Harrisons was the lack of an opportunity to
test the two processes under long-run production conditions. They had
made a number of proving runs under test conditions and, indeed, had
printed more than one engraved issue for other administrations, but this
was the first time they had had an issue using gravure and line engraved
recess 'for real'.

In spite of all the limitations the process imposed on the final design, this
is still a remarkably good issue and one of the more adventurous sets of
stamps of the period.

Social reformers

Social Reformers 1976

On 25 April 1974 the Stamp Advisory Committee was told of a request the Post Office had received from the new Secretary of State at the Department of Industry, Anthony Wedgwood Benn, for a set of stamps devoted to Trade Unionism to be issued on 1 May 1975.

Under the new constitution which surrounded the translation of the Post Office from a Ministry under the Crown to a public Corporation, the Minister had no longer any authority over stamp production other than the power to veto an issue if, in his view, it could be the cause of embarassment to the Government. He could not therefore insist that the Post Office should issue stamps on a particular subject. Nevertheless, the Post Office thought it prudent to give his request full consideration.

It was too late to include the issue in the 1975 programme, which had already been approved by the Post Office Board, and there was no good reason (e.g. an appropriate Trades Union Anniversary) for the question to be re-opened and the programme disturbed. The Committee was therefore asked for its views on how this subject could be dealt with in 1976.

From the start the proposal was regarded with some apprehension, for it was seen, rightly or wrongly, more as an attempt to please the Unions than as a desire to commemorate their historic role in industrial affairs. The fact, too, that there was no appropriate date that year to justify such an issue without departing from its own stamp issuing policy could, in the Committee's view, lay the Post Office open to a charge of conniving at a political manoeuvre. On the other hand, the Committee was in no way averse to acknowledging the place of Trade Unionism in the social pattern, provided that a suitable occasion could be found to justify the issue. After all, the Post Office found no difficulty in commemorating the centenary of the TUC in 1968 with the issue of a stamp.

The Committee spent a considerable amount of time discussing possible frameworks into which Trade Unionism could be fitted with little or no political significance one way or the other. Getting nowhere very fast, it took the unprecedented step of asking for a research study to be undertaken into the whole question of pioneering, reform, and social development, so that a design brief could be written for the subsequent design.

I therefore commissioned Rosalind Dease, a skilful designer as well as a knowledgeable researcher, to prepare a report, together with Alan Martin-Harvey, a one time copywriter and historian, who had been doing a considerable amount of writing for us about stamp issues.

Although, in the end, these research studies may not have contributed a great deal to David Gentleman's ultimate design, they did enable the

Committee and the Post Office to see what the issue was all about.

The editorial pattern, as it were, emerged quite simply. The Post Office would embark on a series of stamp issues under the broad heading of British Pioneering. The first issue would have a sub-heading of Social Reformers and would embrace those reformers who had had a significant effect on social life. The Trade Union content in this first issue tended to dictate the period, for it had been agreed at the start that whatever else was covered by the issue, Trade Unionism would be a significant component.

In the end, it was agreed that only one stamp in the issue of four should be devoted to Trade Unionism, by the inclusion of Thomas Hepburn the Northumberland miners' leader; the other three were to represent other reformers – Elizabeth Fry, Robert Owen and Lord Shaftesbury.

Recently I spoke to David Gentleman about this issue.

SR: 'Of all the stamp issues you have been involved in, Social Reformers was, I suspect, the most taxing, but in many respects the most interesting and the results were quite outstanding. The brief, I recall, was a bit confusing. How did you react to this whole problem at the start?'

DG: 'With enthusiasm, because I believe Trade Unionism is a very important historic force. There was a lot of interesting archival material one could make use of or one could think of more personal ways to suggest what Trade Unionism was all about. In fact I embarked on it by taking several ideas to a sufficiently finished state to see how they would have worked out. One of them was to use figures of working men, taken from various engravings and prints in Union archives and from their beautifully designed membership certificates and sheets. I could also have got very nice historical drawings of people in the working clothes of their trades which would have been very pretty, but maybe too illustrative for this task.

Another set was made up of the more abstract concept of shapes treated graphically, by the simple basic unit on the first stamp becoming more complex on the second, more complex still on the third and so on; a triangle becoming a hexagon, becoming a dodecahedron, as it were.

In the end I did some designs, which I still think were good, with hands, to suggest that hands are the basic tools that are involved in all work – not only manual but creative, intellectual, hands to write down ideas as well as to lay bricks. It was this trio of ideas that was shown to the Committee. I had photographed children's hands and used them as white hands against dark backgrounds.'

SR: 'There is one point about this sort of stamp and it occurred quite frequently on other issues: the Post Office in the end suggested names of people whom they thought were typical of various aspects of social reform and they were tending that way even when you were thinking only of Trade Unionism. Was this an embarassment for you?'

DG: 'As I remember it the Committee's reaction to the first set of ideas I showed them was coloured by the fact that some members were upset at having a Trade Union set at all. That commission ceased abruptly and I began again on a revised brief and on an entirely new job; to design a set of four stamps related to specific pioneer reformers. Trade Unionism was to be included in the form of one early Trade Unionist. Several were suggested, but in the end it was to be Thomas Hepburn, a miners' leader then quite unknown to me. I cannot remember who chose the other three, Elizabeth Fry, the prison reformer; Robert Owen, a textile mill owner, and Lord Shaftesbury. I think the set that was finally issued was harder to justify on grounds of logic, being a more arbitrary choice of people, drawn from a fairly wide field. In terms of national historic importance, the relatively obscure figure of Thomas Hepburn stuck out like a sore thumb.'

Social reformers

SR: 'In graphic terms it was a complete departure from any other issue you had done. Did the subject take hold, as it were, and did you find it leading you along these almost abstract lines and away from what, in your earlier issues, had been more pictorial?'

DG: 'Yes it did, and the particular graphic approach began to grow quite indefinably in the course of thinking about it, and on the whole I don't wish I had done it in any other way. I realized that by making the fact that stamps are repeated on the printed sheet the basis of the idea, I could suggest the contrast between the human scale of the people involved, and the monumental, all-embracing nature of the evils that the social reformers were concerned to put right. If one could express this by bringing in the old idea of the hands taken from the earlier set of proposals and make those hands – tiny hands – appear on the stamp, but allow the background to them, whether it was the pulleys of Robert Owen's factory or the chains and bars of Elizabeth Fry's prisons, to spread over the whole sheet, it could make an all-enveloping pattern.'

In an interview with *Design* magazine published in the August 1976 issue David Gentleman had this to say of these stamps 'From the outset, hands seemed the best: powerful and evocative, able to suggest the misery and grime, small enough to be dwarfed by machinery or fetters. Hands also let me show the exploitation of children without sentimentality.'

It is of course this incredible capacity for analysis that makes David Gentleman the designer he is. By taking into account the complexity of the subject and forgetting the confusion of the brief, he produced what is perhaps the most imaginative pictorial issue the Post Office has ever published. The stamps stand as classics of intellectual comment and visual expression, although they were, I suppose, the most unpopular stamps ever issued, at least with some people.

9/4 *Top row:* David Gentleman's drawings using the theme of hands at work. *Above:* the machinery theme being developed to incorporate the hands theme

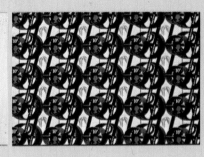

9/5 The Social Reformers final
issue using hands in their social
environment

Silver Jubilee

Silver Jubilee 1977 and 25th Anniversary of the Coronation 1978
I have put these two issues together because in many ways they are
interdependent. When the Post Office started to consider the Silver Jubilee
issue for 1977 it knew that it would be issuing a second set for the
Coronation in the following year. It was essential therefore that the two
events should be kept quite separate and that the Jubilee designs should
not, if at all possible, be seen to be commemorating the Coronation. The
fact that the two occasions did not fall within the same year gave an added
significance to the Accession, which in the past had tended to be overshadowed by the Coronation itself.

Three designers were commissioned, two of them Jeffery Matthews and
Peter Hatch, on a completely open brief; and the third William Gardner,
to explore the possibility of basing a set on the Great Seals of the realm.

Jeffery Matthews submitted four possible sets using Arnold Machin's
definitive portrait; a new drawn portrait of his own and two based on
Edmund Dulac's 1953 Coronation portrait; and two sets based on royal
heraldic devices, such as the St Edward's Crown, the Royal Coat of Arms,
the Royal Standard and the Badge of the House of Windsor.

Peter Hatch concentrated on photographs of the Accession, the Coronation and some of the Queen's first official visits in the United Kingdom.

Of all the preliminary designs submitted, the heraldic sets by Jeffery
Matthews were the most promising. What we did not anticipate at the time
we started to develop one of them was the sheer impossibility of finding four
appropriate symbols which would bind the set together visually. The
problem was further aggravated by our determination not to fall into the
trap of commemorating the wrong event by using pictorial elements
proper to the Coronation but not the Accession.

With hindsight maybe we were all a bit obstinate in being reluctant to
admit defeat, for Jeffery Matthews did a prodigious amount of work in his
search for a solution.

In spite of many hours with Garter King of Arms and Windsor Herald,
both of whom had tried desperately to help us out of our trouble, we failed
to find a way out of this tangle and so sadly had to abandon a brilliant idea.

But now time was beginning to run out. All the to-ing and fro-ing over
the heraldic problems had taken a large slice out of the programme and so
far we had not yet a viable set in sight. Jeffery Matthews started again on a
photographic solution and Peter Hatch worked on a set of portraits of
Queens of England, but although they looked very nice as an issue seen
together, to have only one stamp bearing the reigning monarch's portrait
would not have been acceptable for such a significant occasion. Almost in

desperation I commissioned Richard Guyatt, Professor of Graphic Design at the Royal College of Art, to design a non-heraldic, non-Coronation set, relying solely on graphic decoration in the manner of his work for Wedgwood.

In due course he came up with a basic design, with variations in detail and colour, to make up the set. Back we went to the Palace to see Sir Martin Charteris. The Queen approved the general approach, but alas could give no sittings for Richard Guyatt to draw his new portrait. The Palace, however, supplied him with numerous photographs, which was the best that could be done in the time.

It was an arduous job, but in the end it worked, and a lot of the work Jeffery Matthews had done on some of his Jubilee designs became the starting point for his Coronation Anniversary issue a year later.

Peter Hatch and Roger Denning were also commissioned to submit designs for the Coronation set and it is interesting to see the similarity of approach between all three designers. The issued stamps had a great dignity about them and they may rank as one of the more distinguished sets of stamps of the reign.

I asked Jeffery Matthews whether he felt inhibited, when thinking about the Jubilee, by the Coronation Anniversary the following year.

JM: 'I don't think it worried me unduly because I tend, as with all design problems, to take things a step at a time. Even if I had thought about the Coronation I would most probably have seen it as somebody else's problem! But as we were concentrating only on the Accession it seemed appropriate that I should look to the historic background of the Queen.'

SR: 'What took you to the heraldic approach in the first place?'

JM: 'The memory of what actually happened in 1952. The Heralds reading the Proclamation, the thing seeming very heraldic. I remember it as a tiny moment of pageantry, shrouded rather by the death of the King. It was all a bit of a contradiction really, because, after a period of mourning, we all started to look forward to the Coronation in the following June. In a way that's what I did with these stamps, taking the heraldic bits of the Coronation, and trying to make them into a consistent and acceptable set.'

SR: 'But what of the 25th anniversary of the Coronation itself?'

JM: 'Peter Shrives asked me quite specifically to pick up the threads again from one of the Jubilee sets I had submitted, which showed the Regalia in a more stylized way, using part elevation drawings. As somebody said – I had re-introduced the half-crown stamp! I also felt that for this occasion the Queen herself should be given far more prominence and I

The Silver Jubilee of The Queen's Accession

9/6 Preliminary designs: *above*, William Gardner's design based on one of the Seals of the Realm; *left*, Jeffery Matthews's submissions based on the Badge of the House of Windsor and the Royal Coat of Arms; *bottom*, Peter Hatch's set of Queens of England

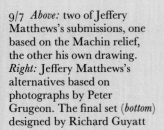

9/7 *Above:* two of Jeffery Matthews's submissions, one based on the Machin relief, the other his own drawing. *Right:* Jeffery Matthews's alternatives based on photographs by Peter Grugeon. The final set (*bottom*) designed by Richard Guyatt

Coronation

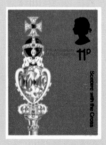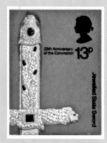

9/8 *Above:* designs submitted by Jeffery Matthews for the Coronation issue. *Left:* Peter Hatch's submissions. *Below:* drawings prepared by Roger Denning. *Opposite:* finished artwork for Jeffery Matthews's accepted set with the issued stamps

quite deliberately made her head fairly large. I also used the toned head, which looks younger and which is uncrowned and this helped to create a rather nostalgic view of twenty-five years ago. The fact that the rest of the stamp, being printed in gold, is rather elusive – it comes and goes as you move it – made the Queen's head the most dominant unchanging feature and gave her the pre-eminence she deserved. That pleased me.'

Epilogue

These four issues do more for me than explain the diverse nature of the problem of postage stamp design, for they typify the great variety of interests and the constant excitement which made my time at the Post Office so stimulating.

Whether it was the sheer joy of watching drawings, like those of the Village Churches, grow and flower; or trying to beat the production problems of Sailing; or the well-nigh intractable political arguments surrounding Social Reformers; or, for all its early disappointments, making in the end a worthy contribution to the Silver Jubilee celebrations. They all, in their own way, combined to create a rare experience that I shall always remember with great pride and much gratitude.

List of designers

The stamps and essays, as well as the archival material from the Phillips Collection in the National Postal Museum, London, are reproduced by courtesy of The Post Office.

Index

College of Arts &
Community Studies

Eastwood Lane, Rotherham S65 1EG
Telephone: 61801